I0491317

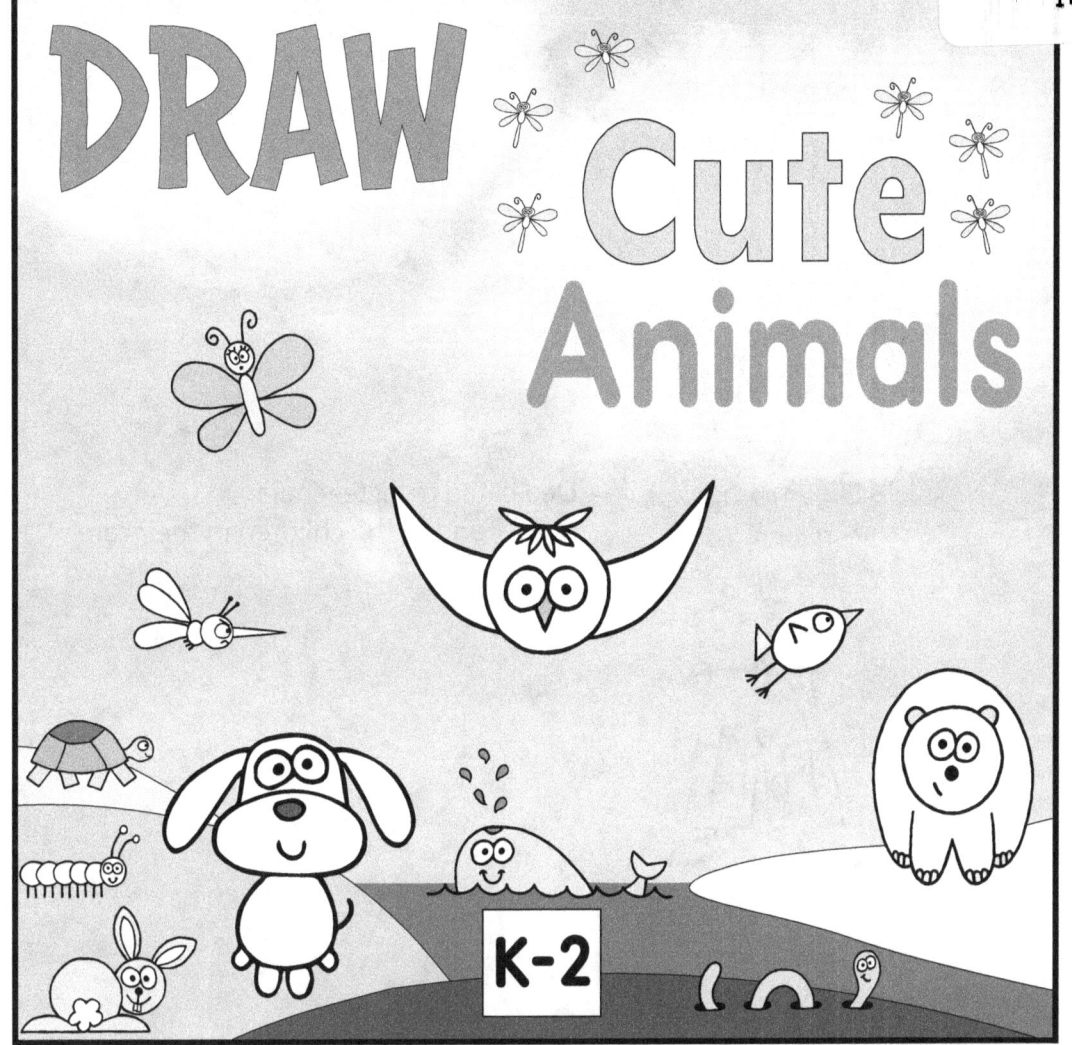

by

Mark Linley

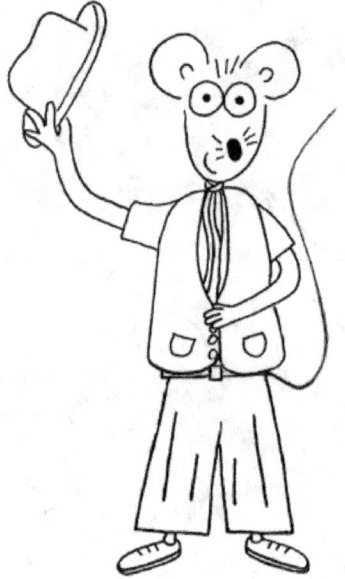

Dedicated to all teachers
and to the children in their care

ISBN 978-1-952855-01-6

Copyright © 2024 by Mark Linley
All rights reserved by author.
Permission to copy for single classroom use only.
Electronic distribution limited to single classroom use only.

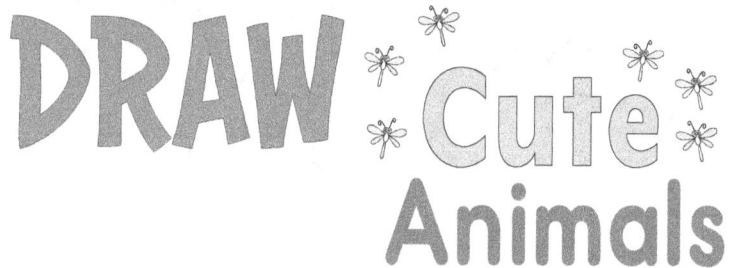

CONTENTS

DIRECTED DRAWING LESSONS

INSTRUCTIONAL GUIDE

MORE

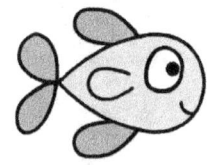

LESSONS

from Easy to Difficult

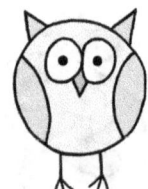
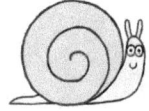
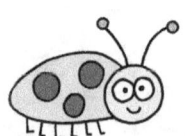
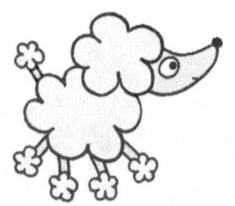

LESSONS

in Alphabetical Order

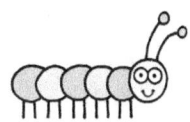
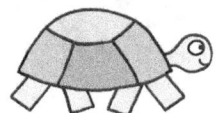

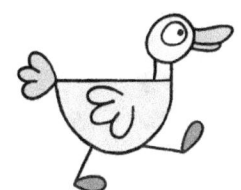

<u>bird</u>

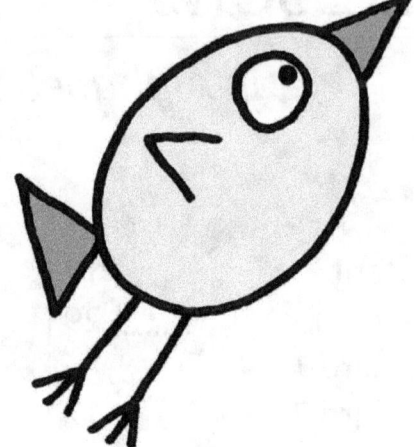

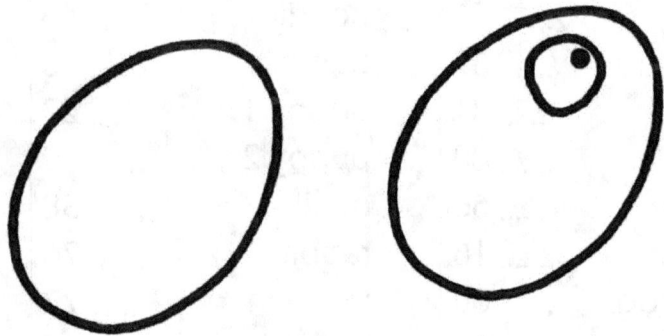

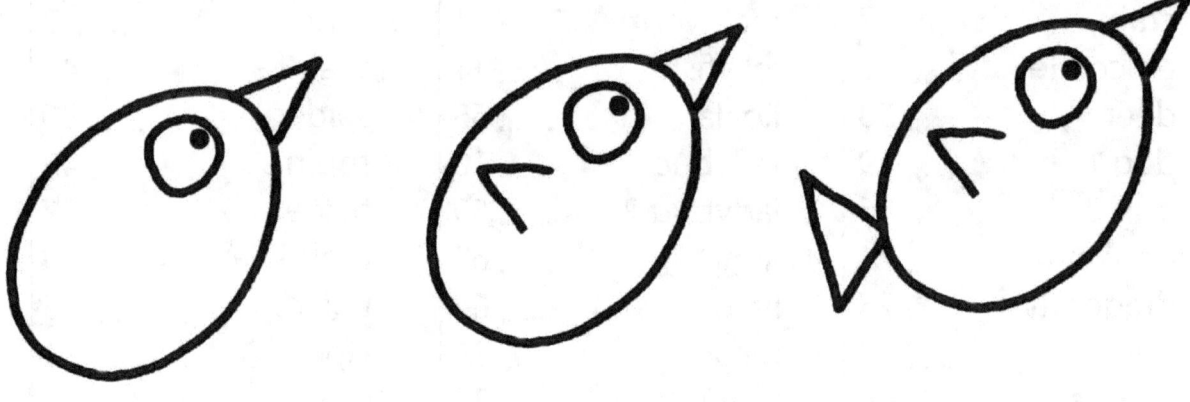

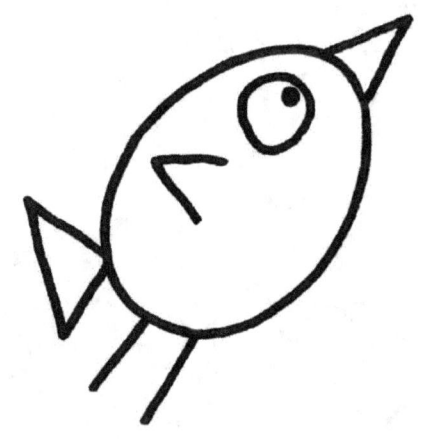

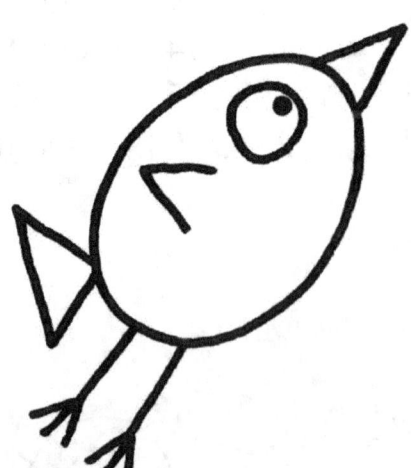

slug

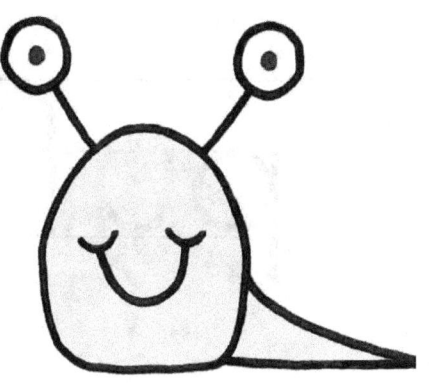

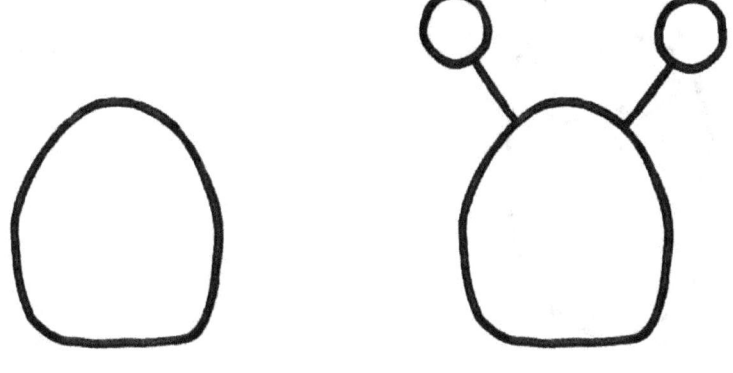

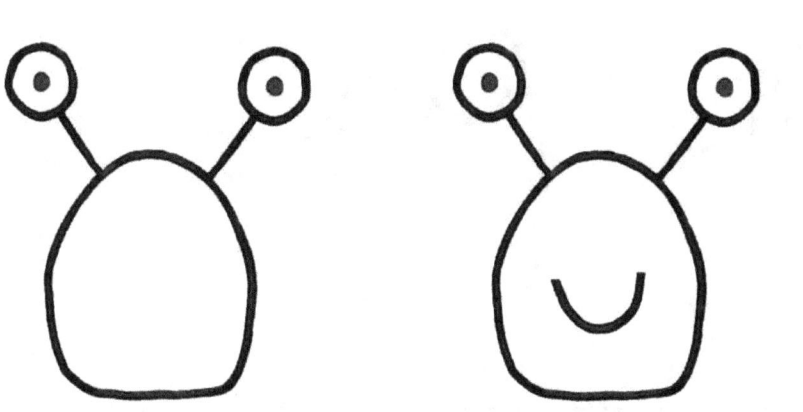

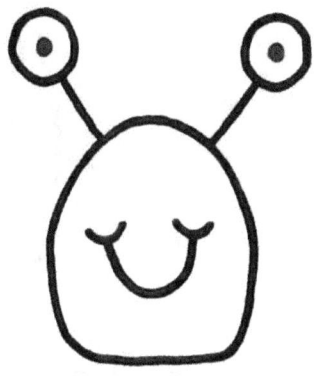

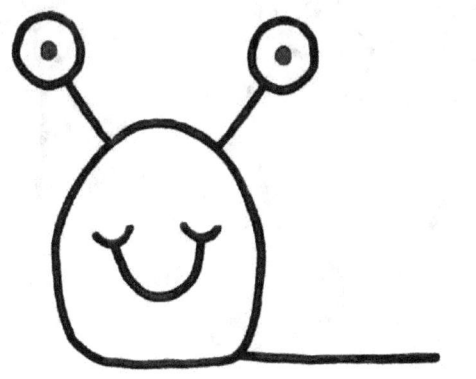

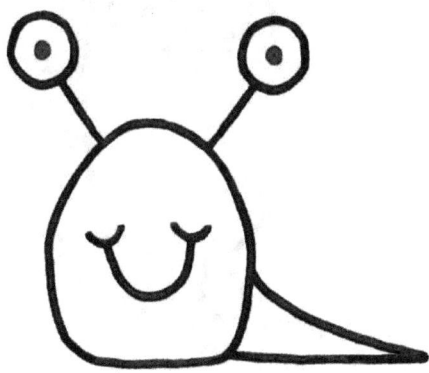

puffin

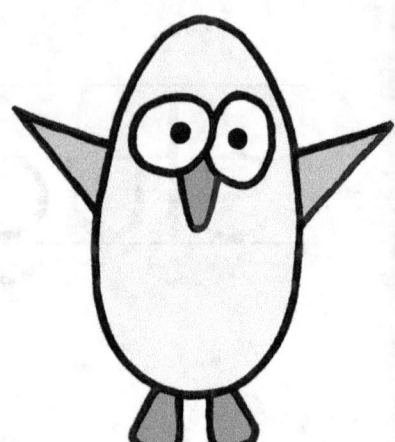

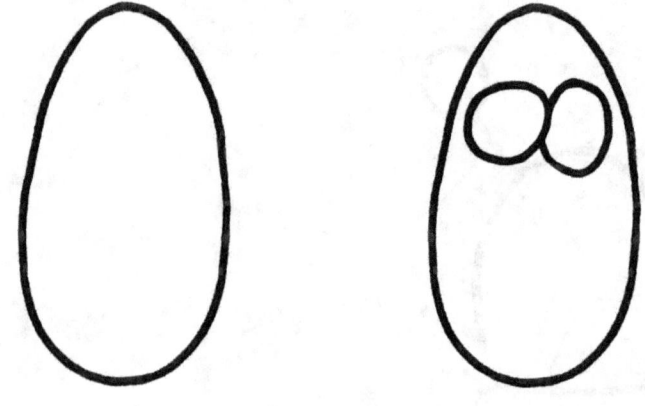

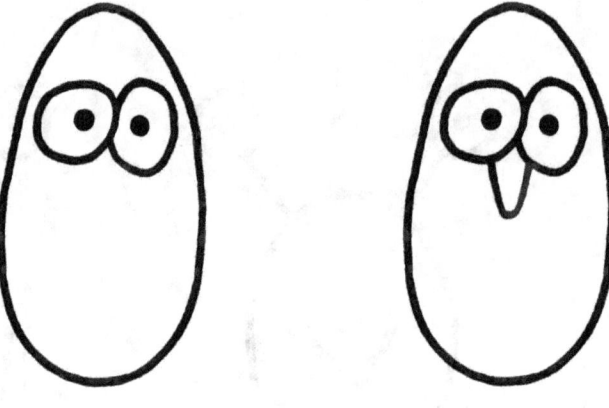

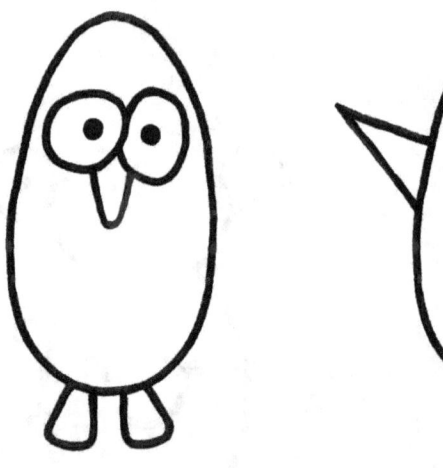
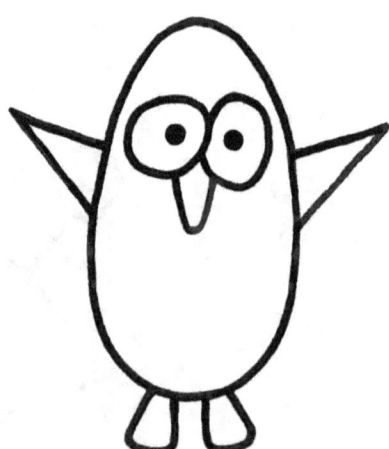

fish

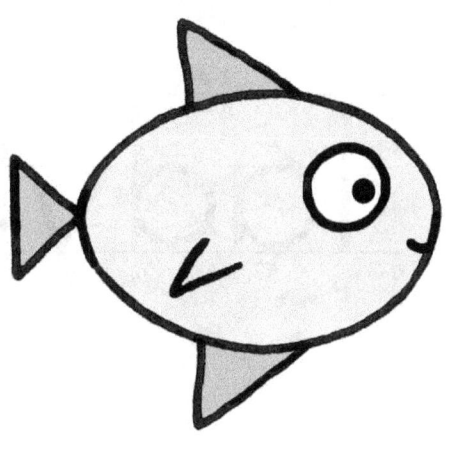

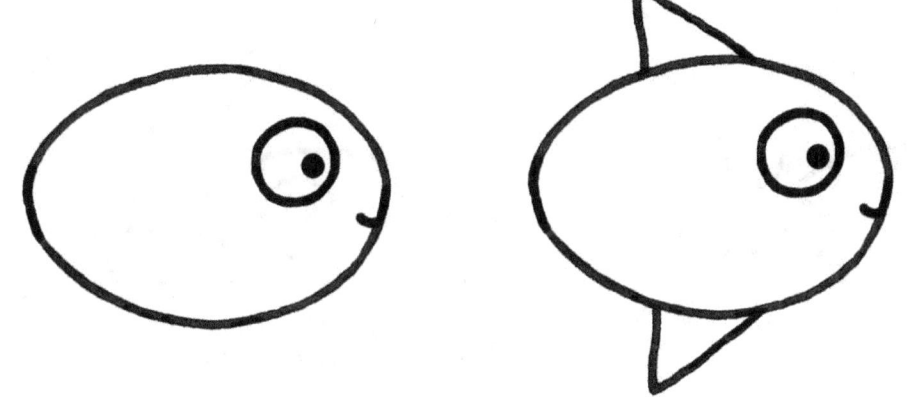

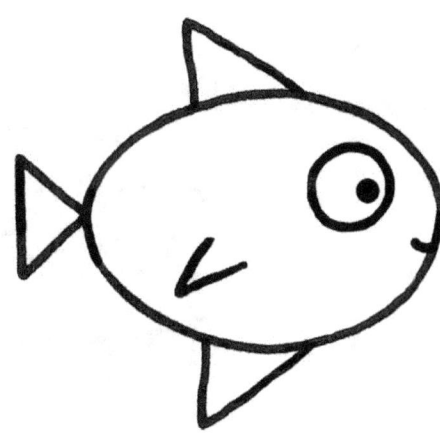

ladybug

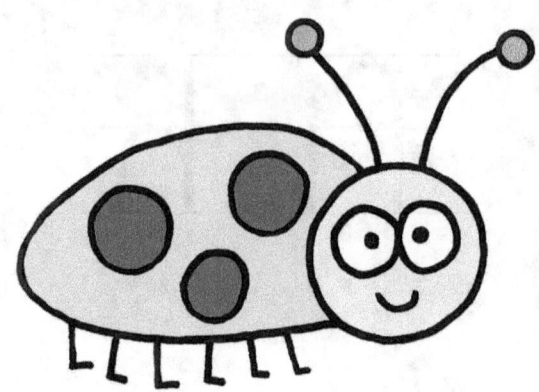

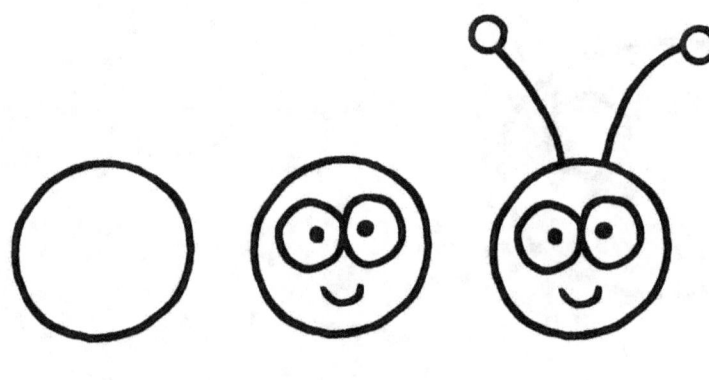

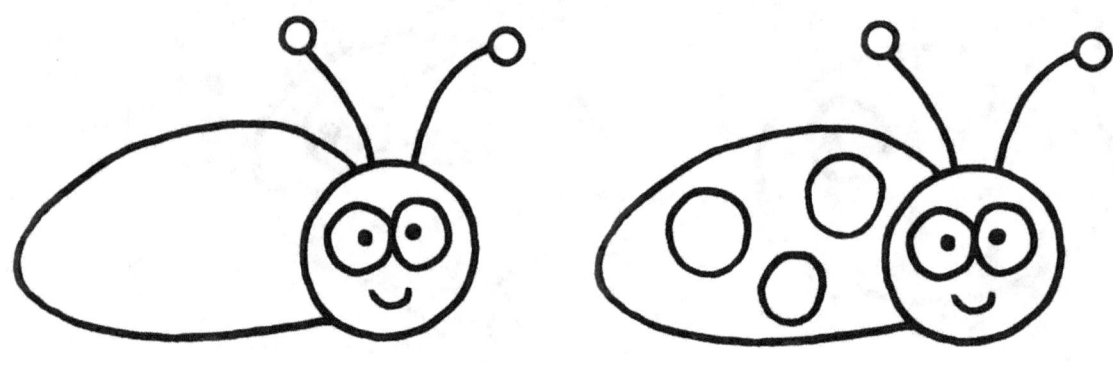

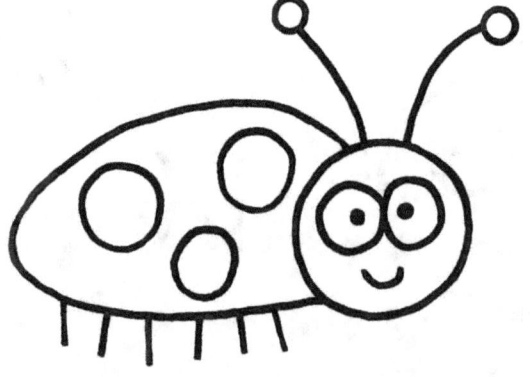

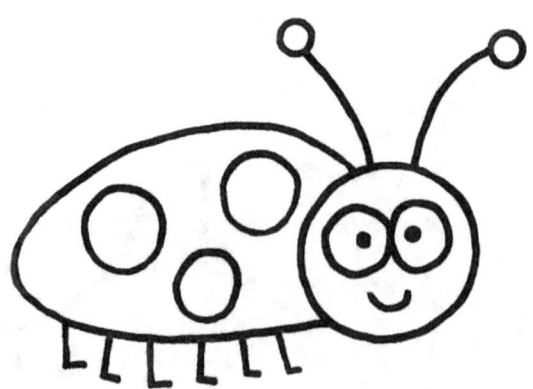

jellyfish

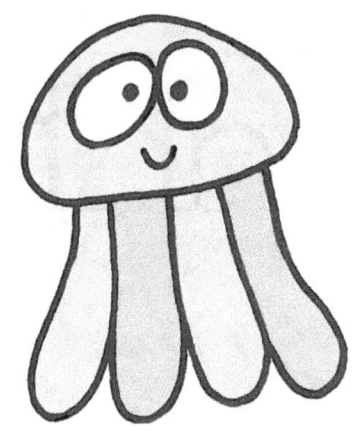

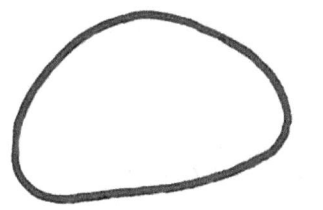
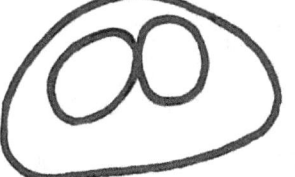

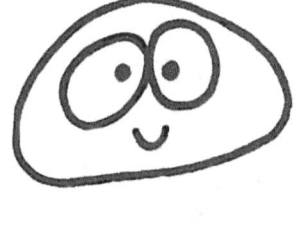
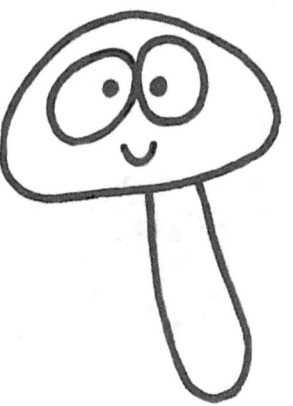
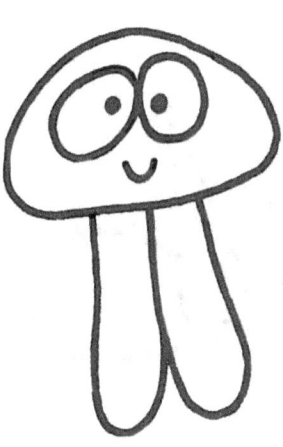

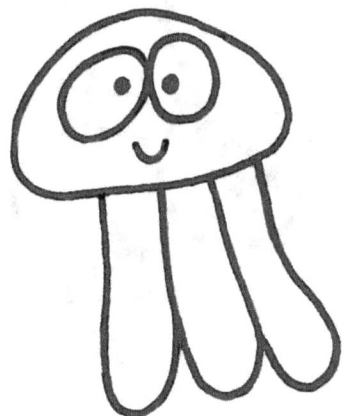
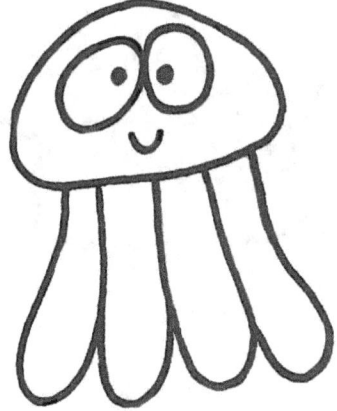

ant

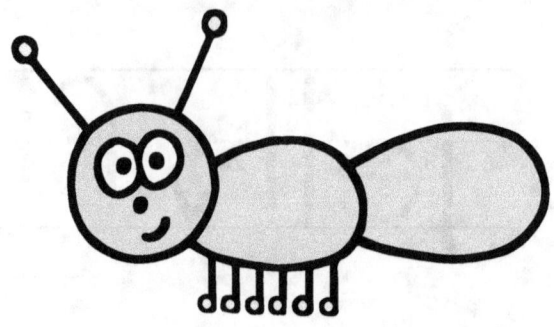

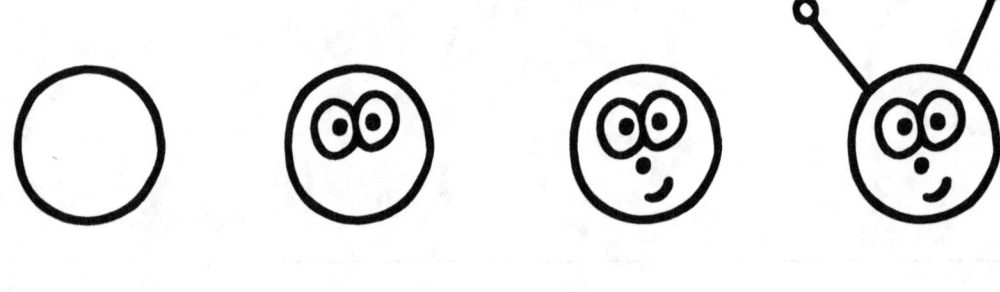

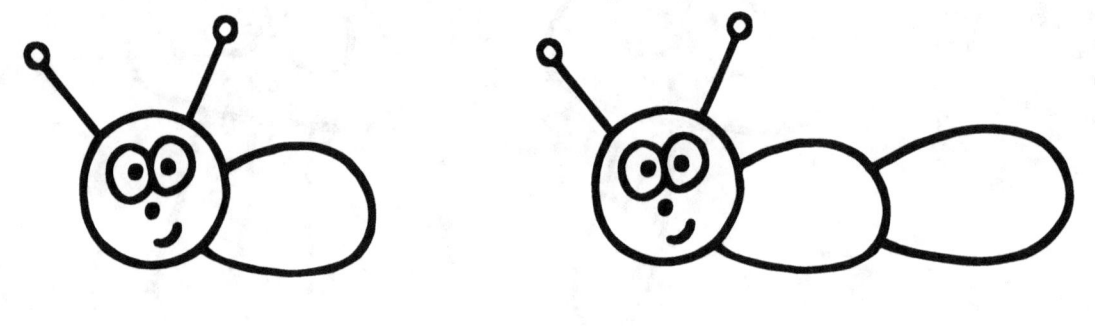

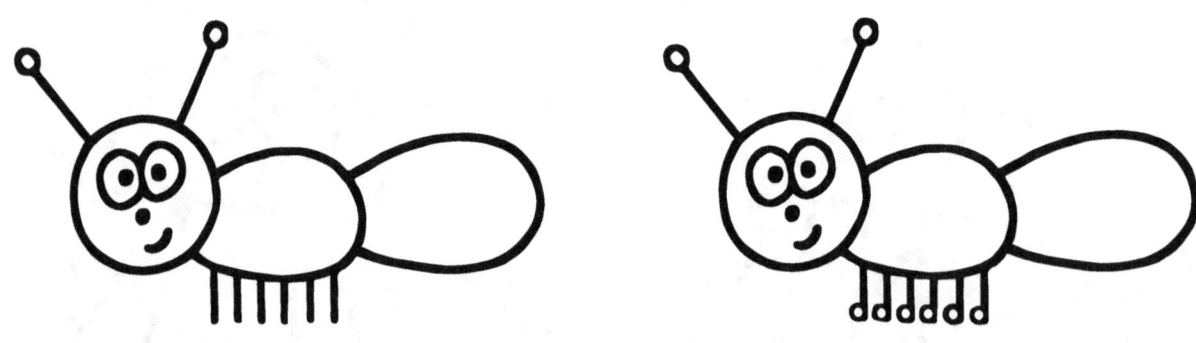

bug

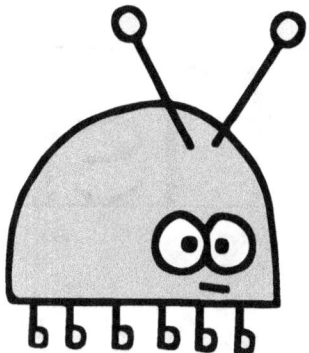

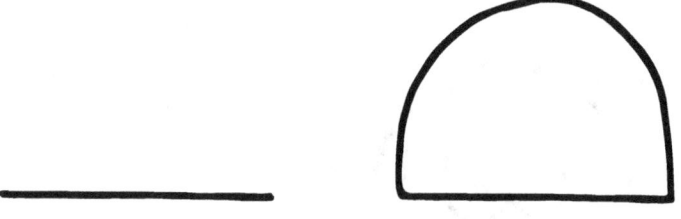

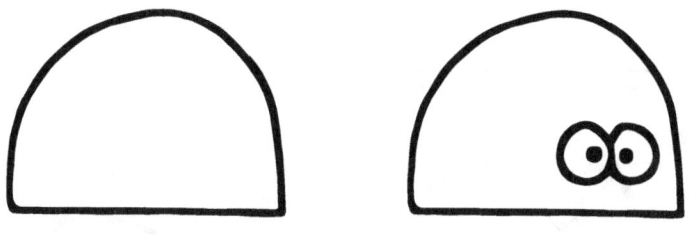

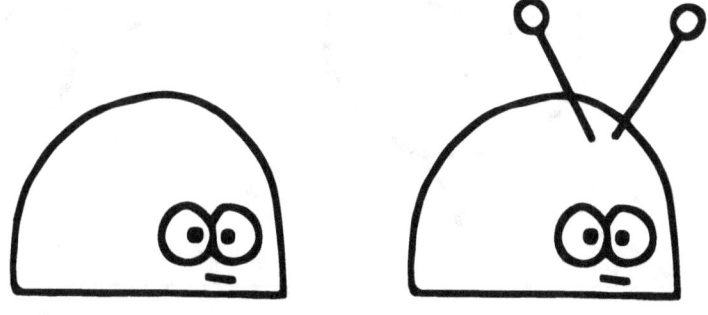

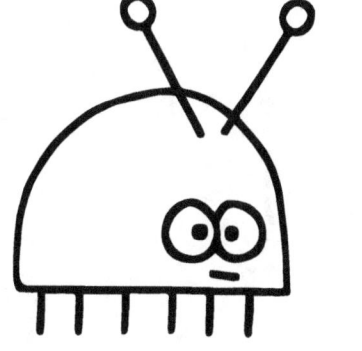
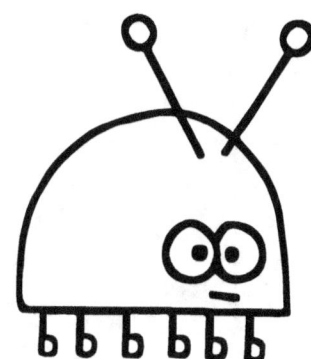

13

fish

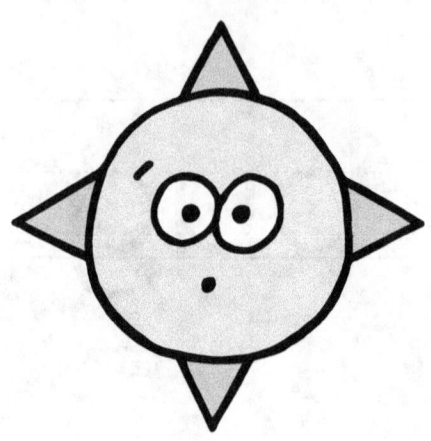

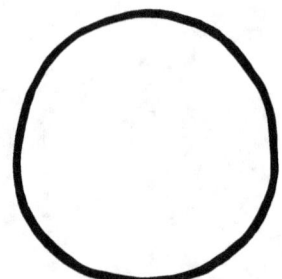
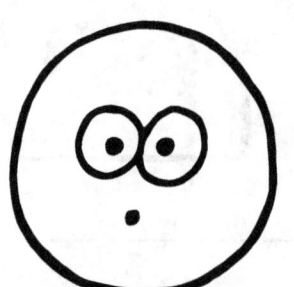

_____

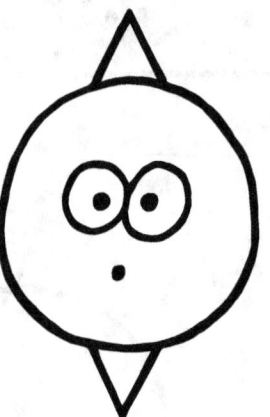
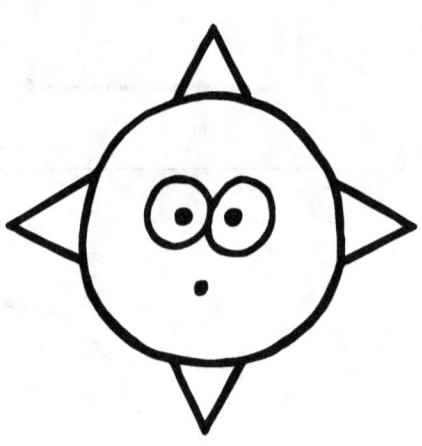

_____

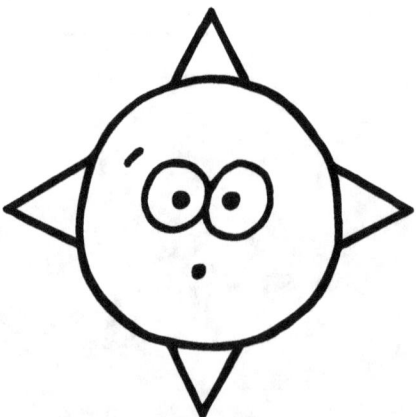

fish

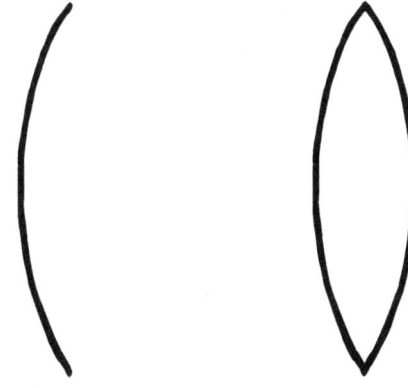

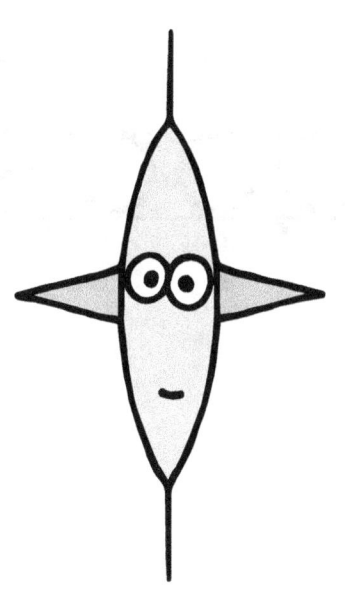

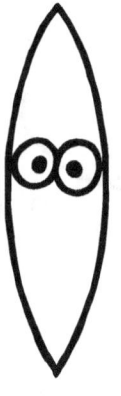 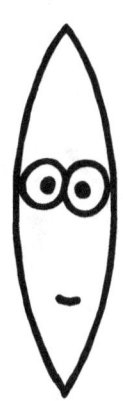

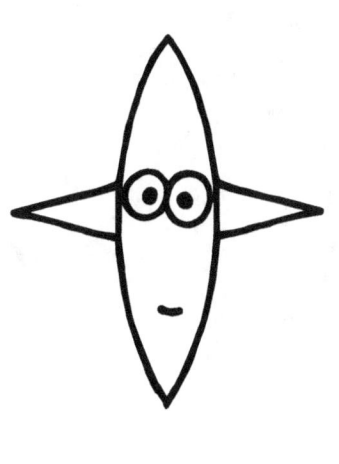 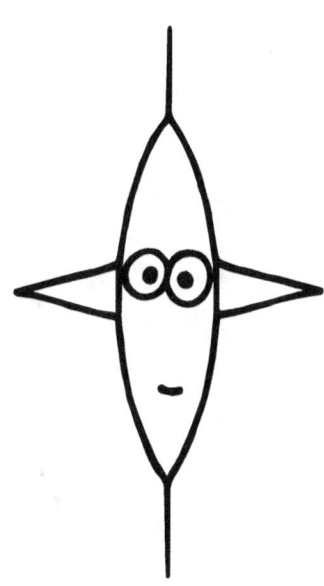

15

goose

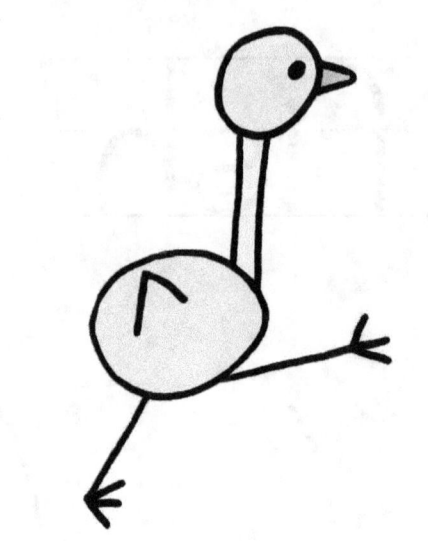

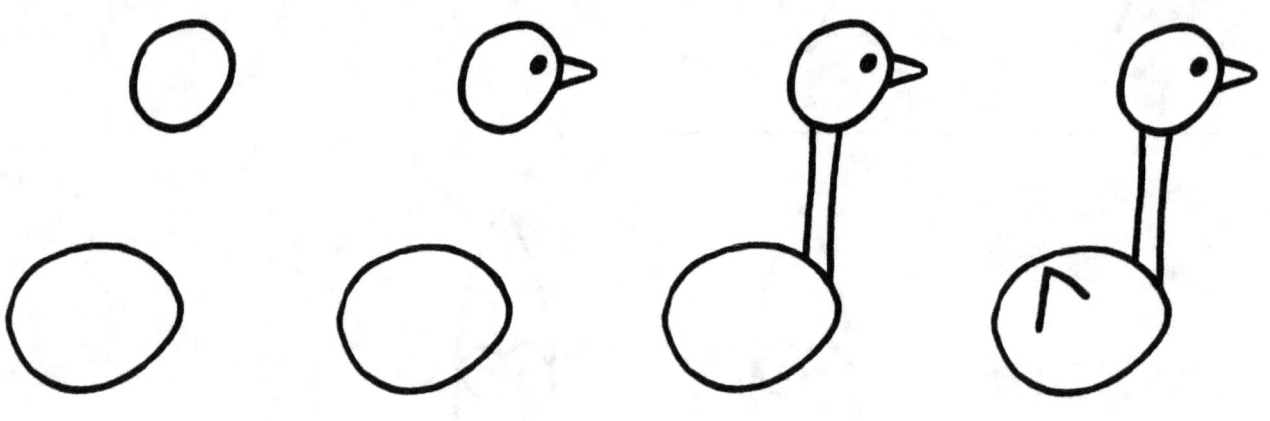

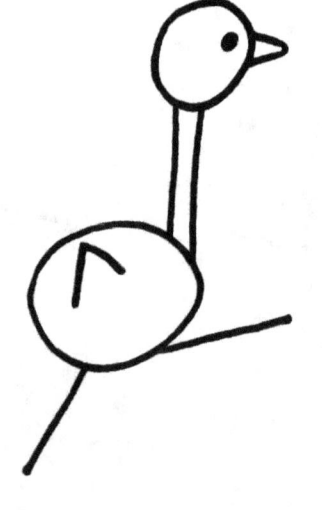

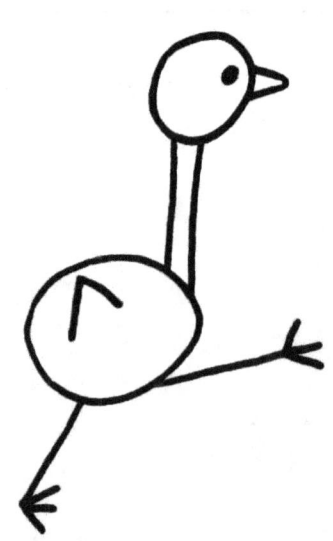

bird

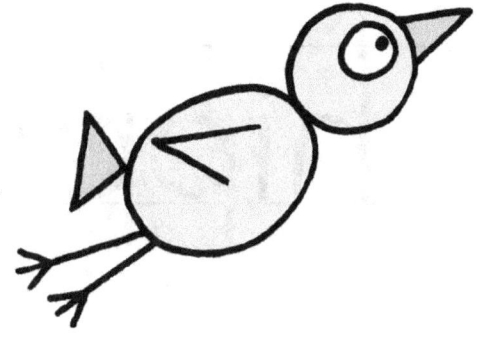

hippo

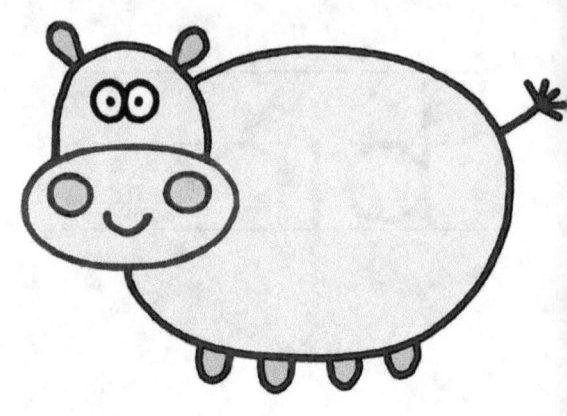

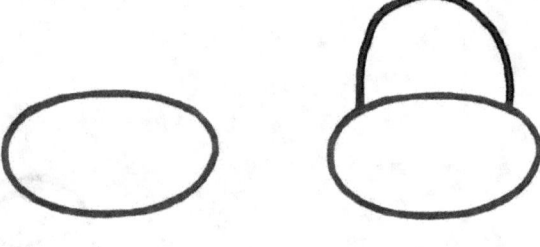
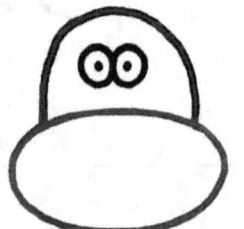

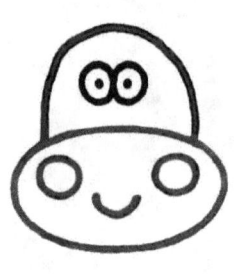
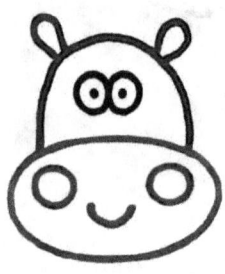
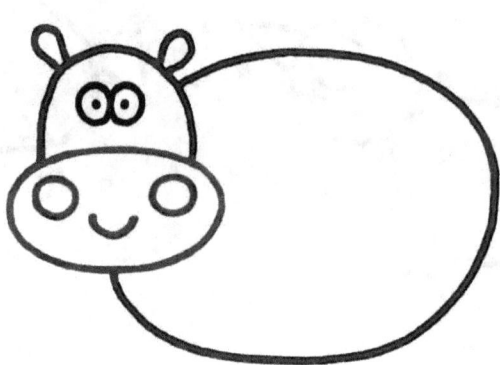

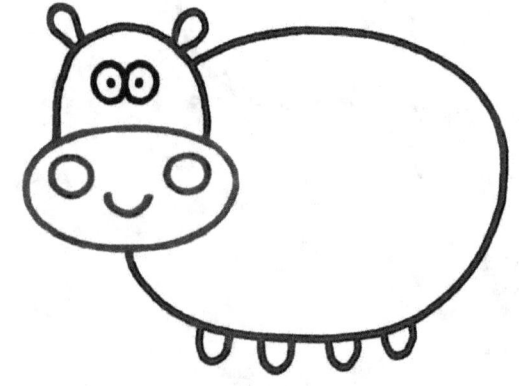
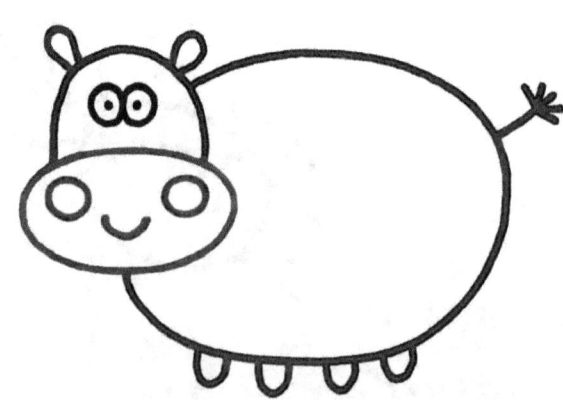

dog

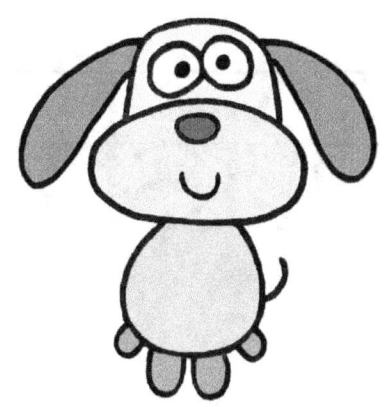

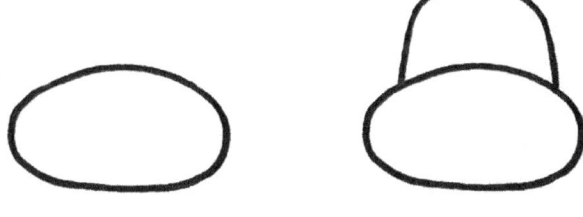

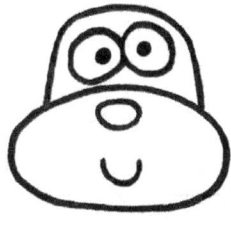 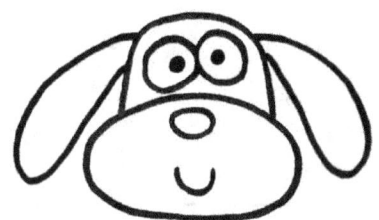

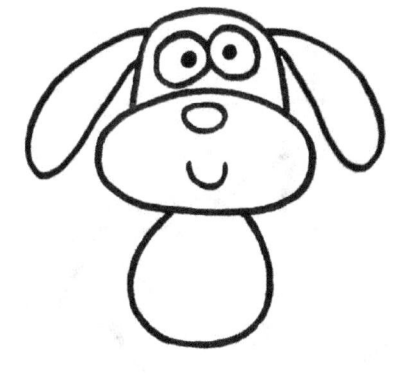 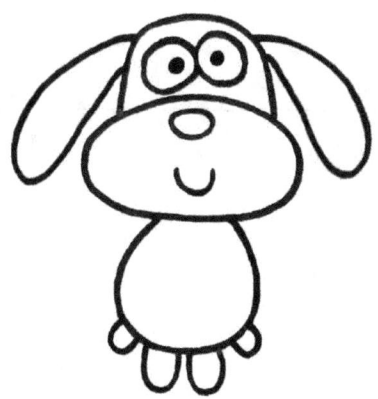 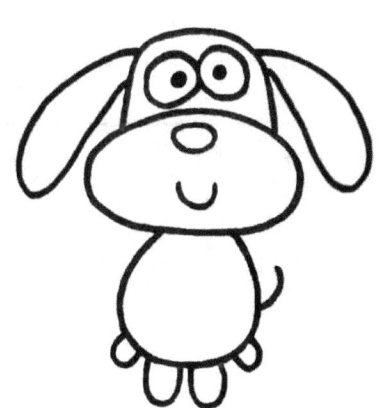

fish

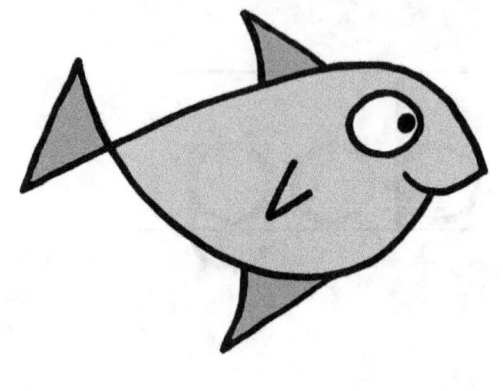

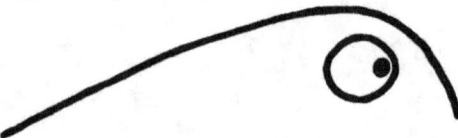

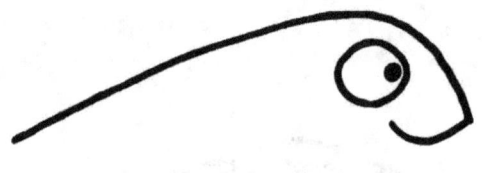

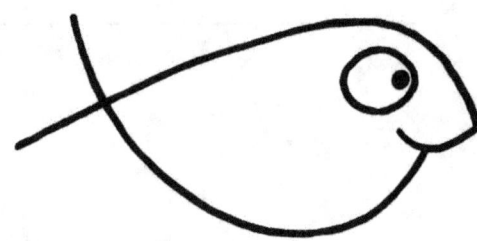

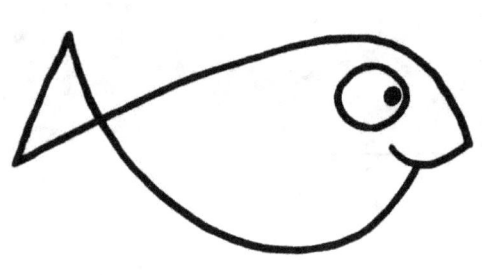

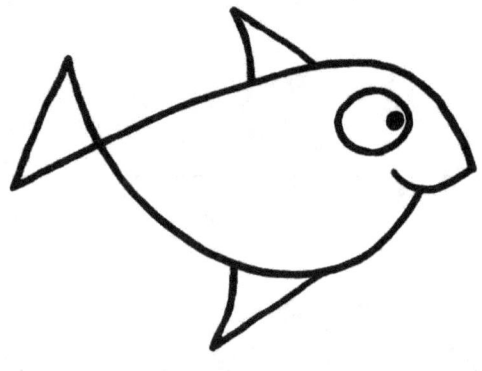

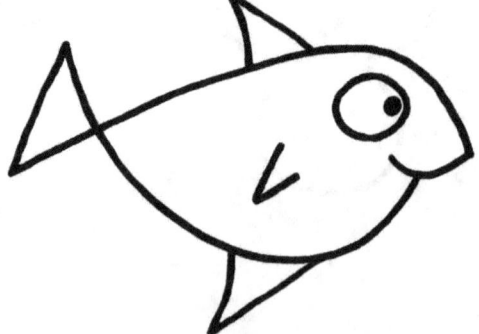

fish

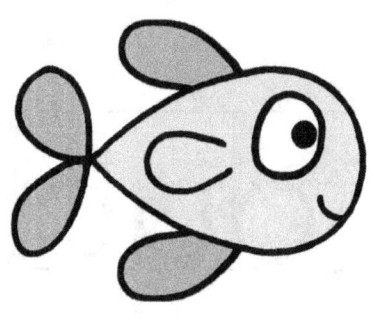

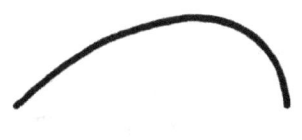

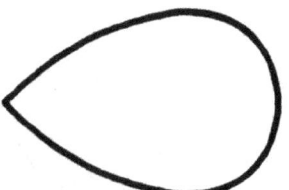

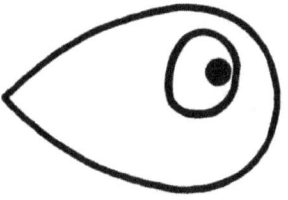

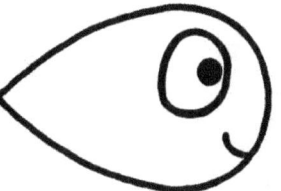

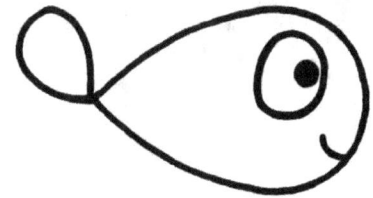

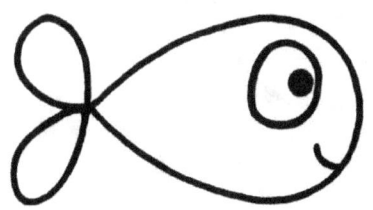

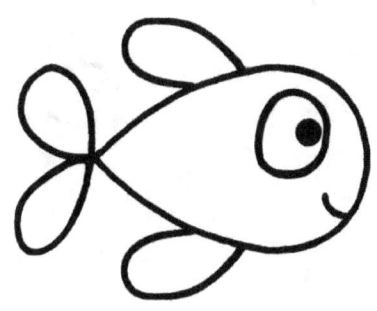

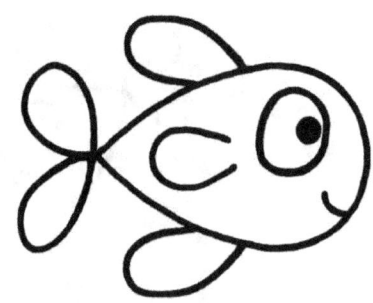

duck

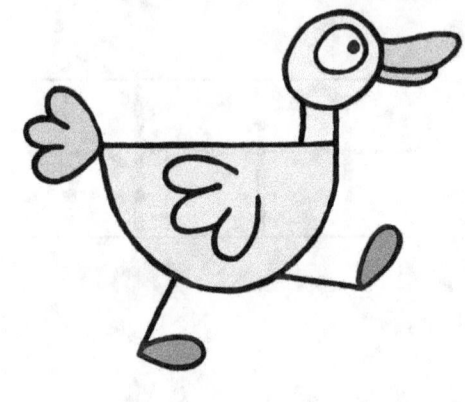

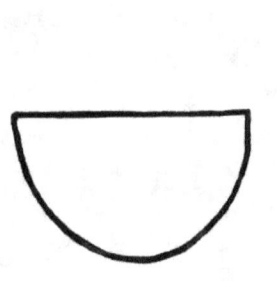
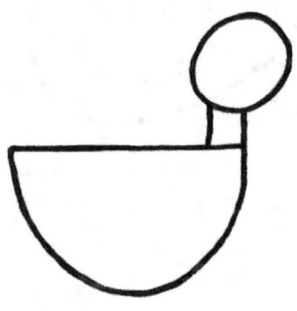
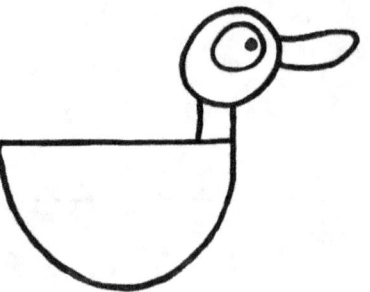

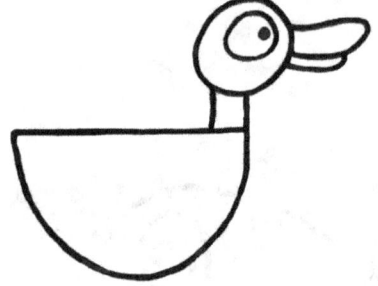
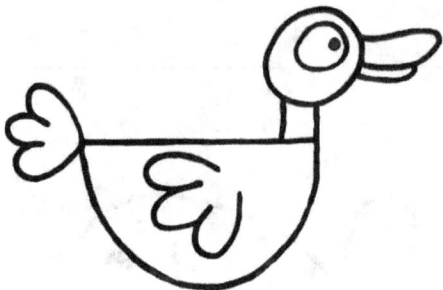

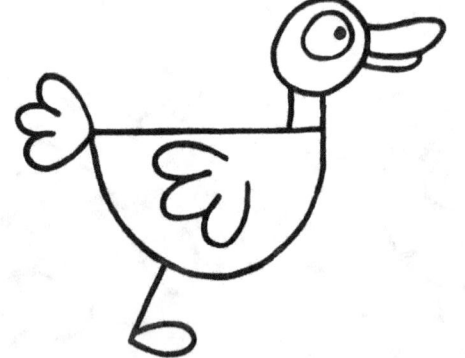
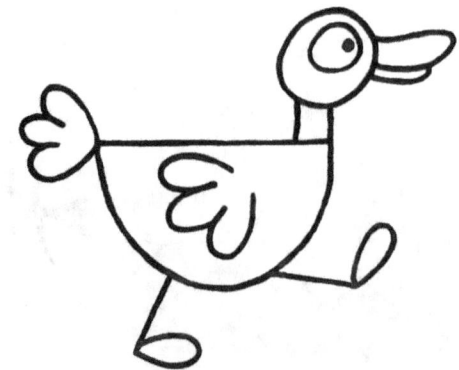

cat

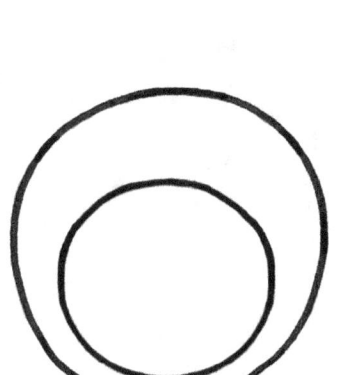 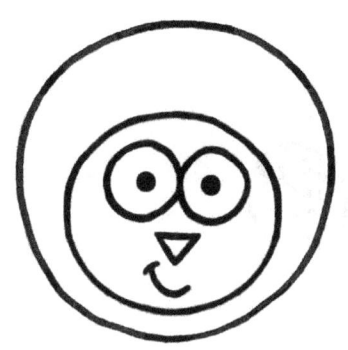 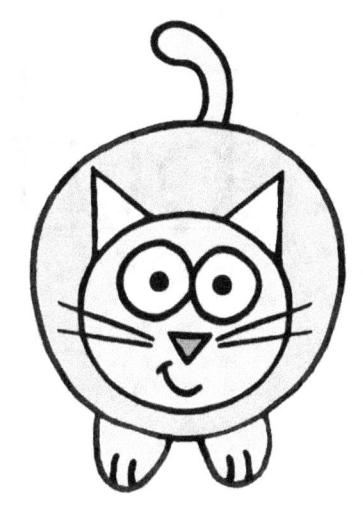

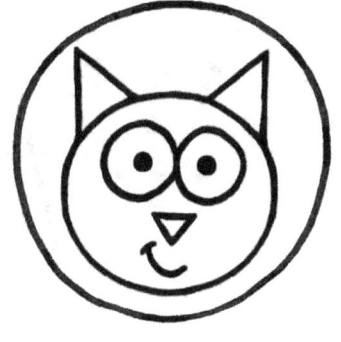 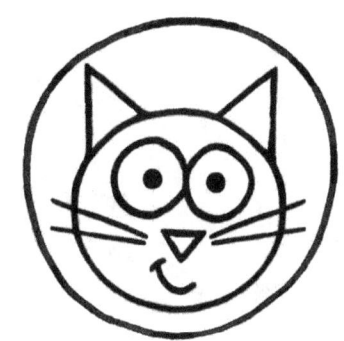

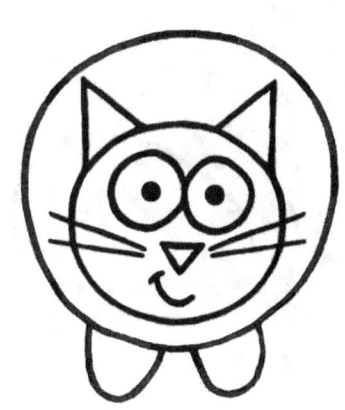 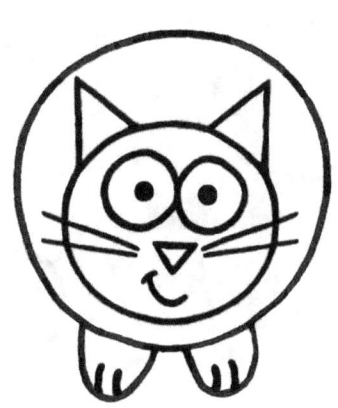 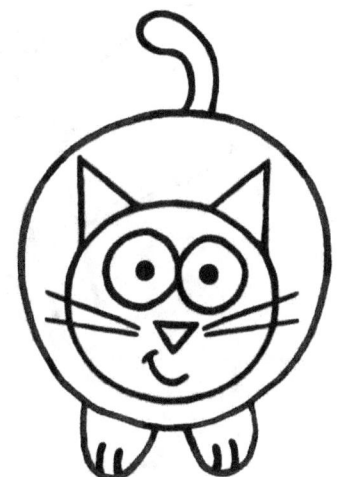

butterfly

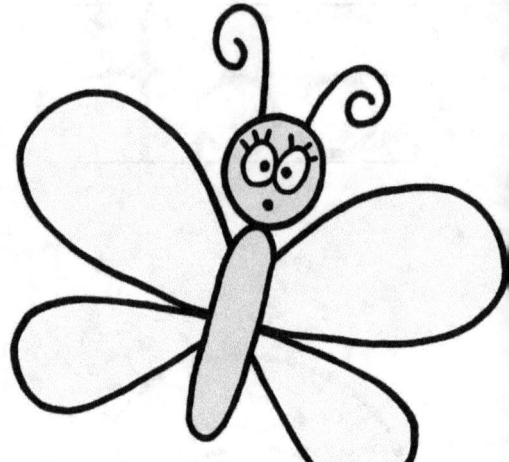

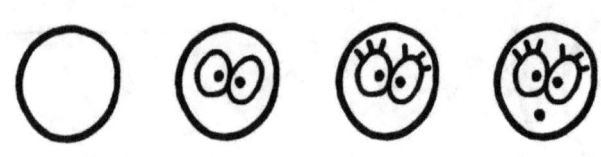

_____

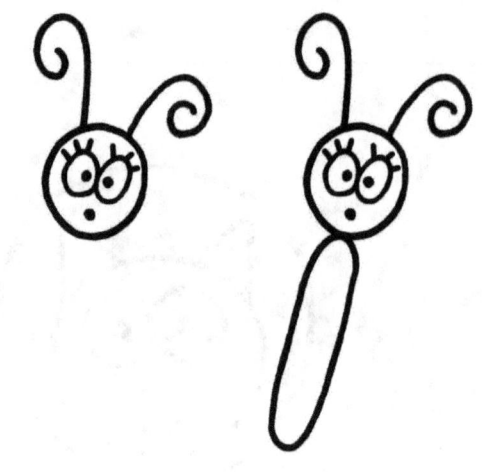

_____

dragonfly

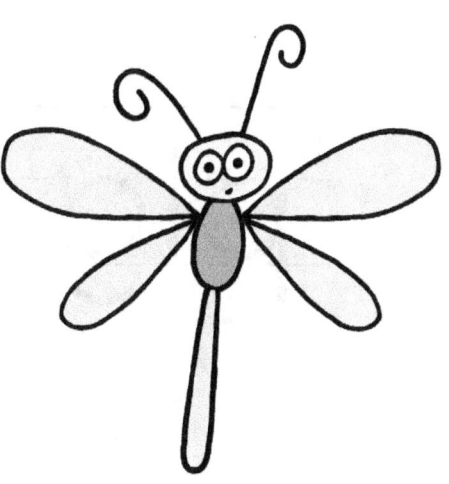

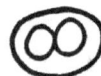 

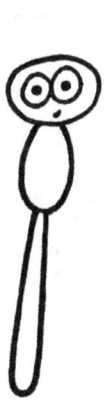 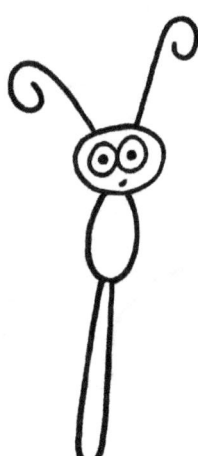

 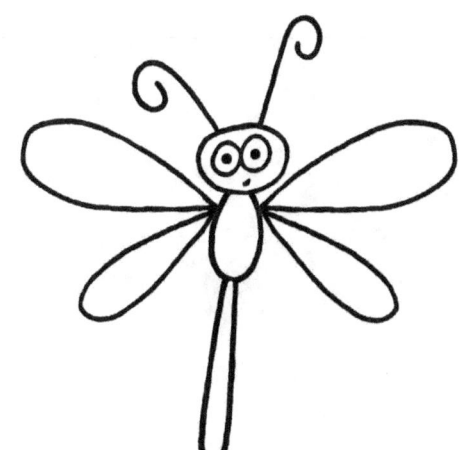

pig

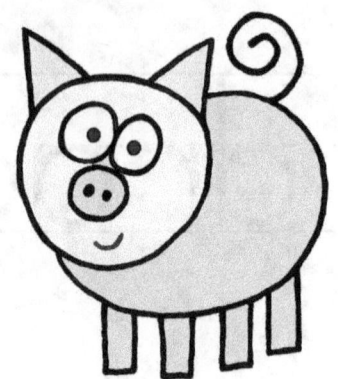

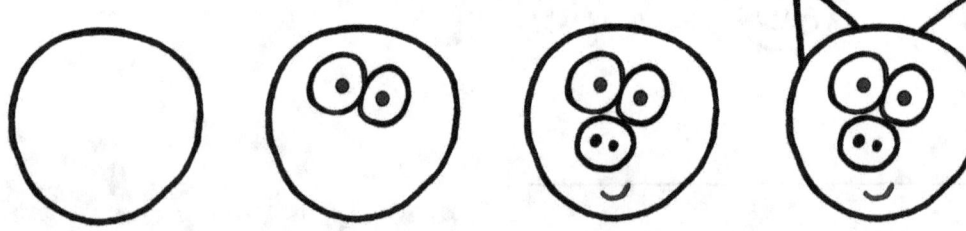

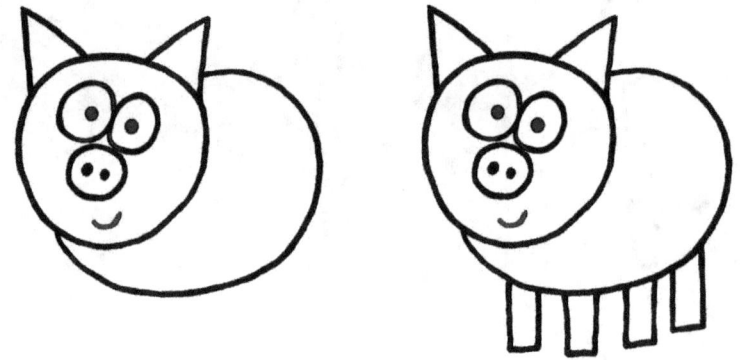

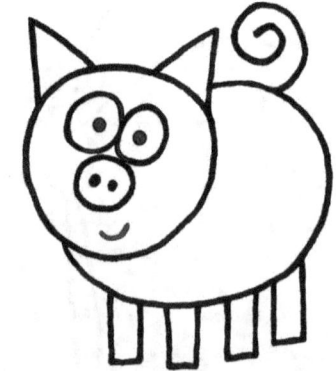

puppy

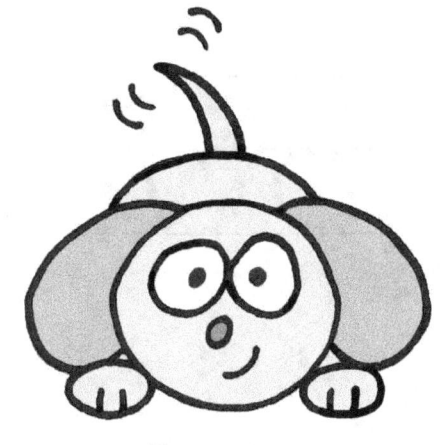

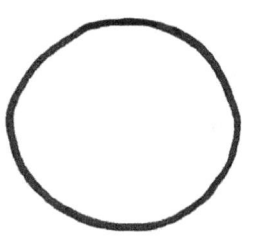 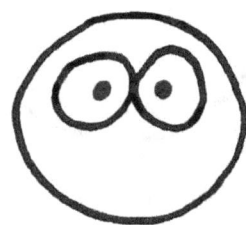 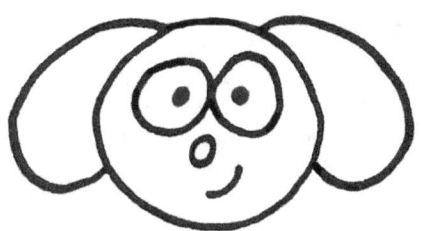

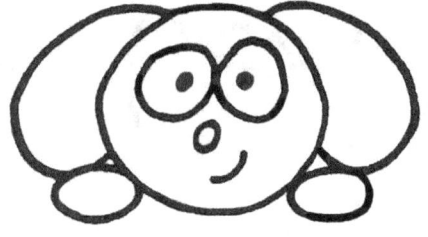 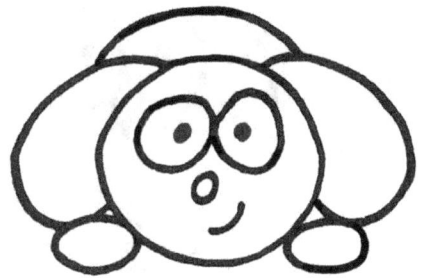

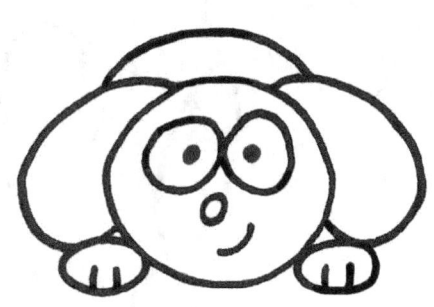 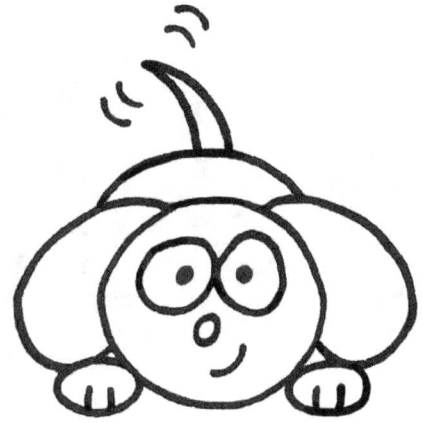

owl

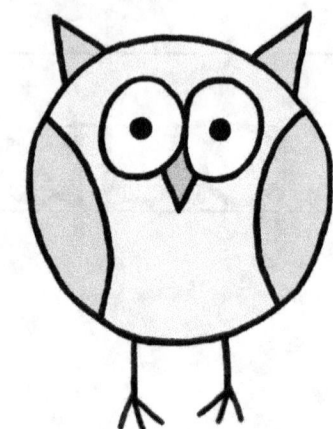

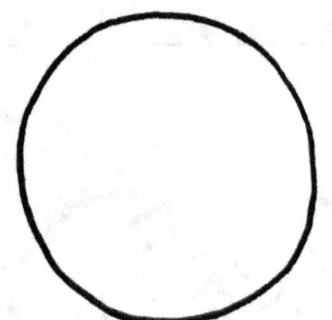
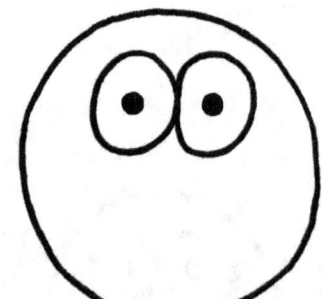

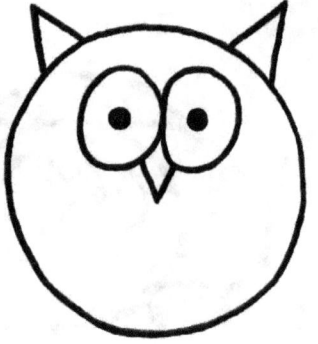
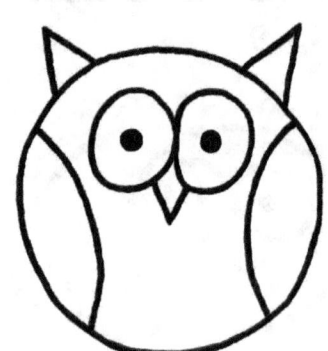

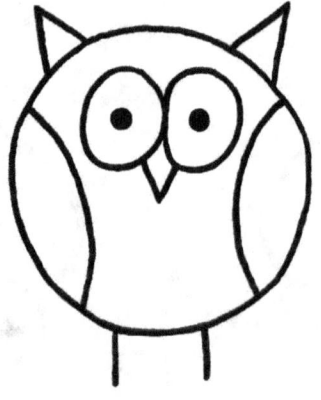
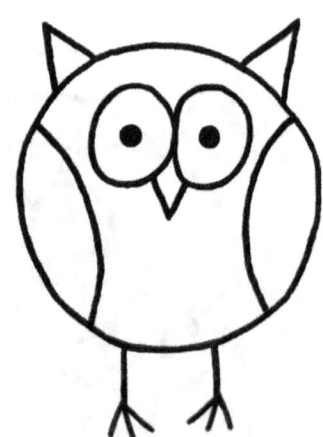

bear

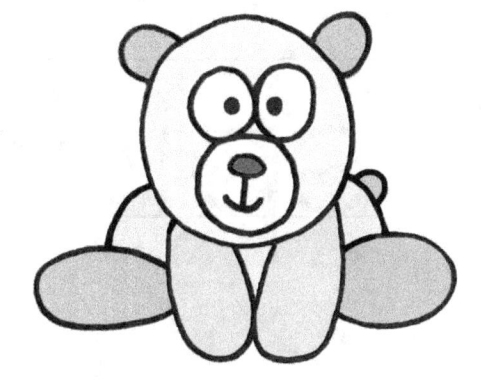

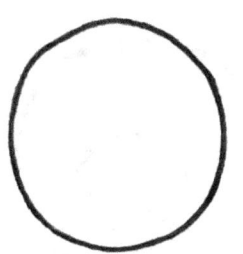 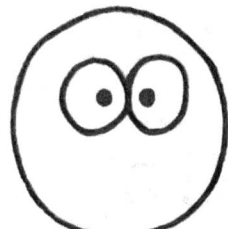 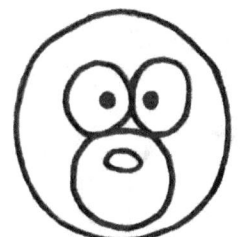

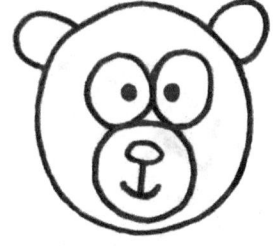 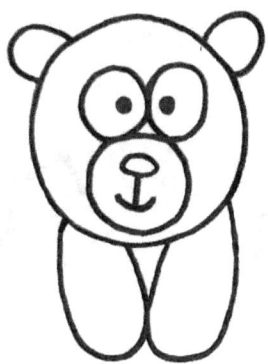 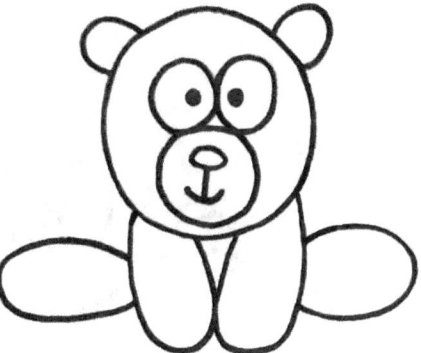

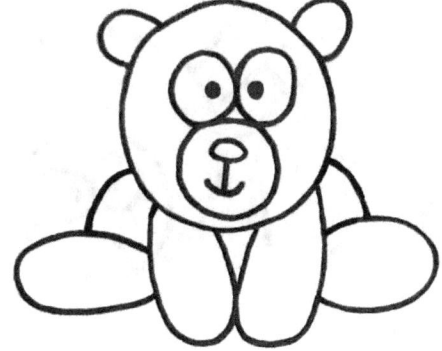 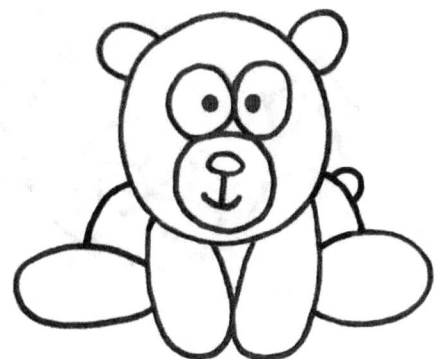

spider

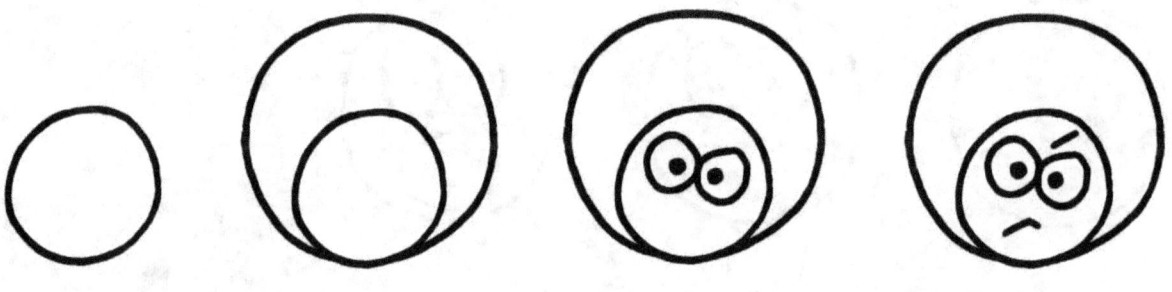

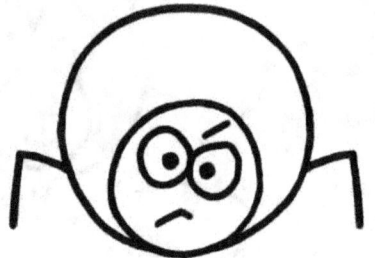 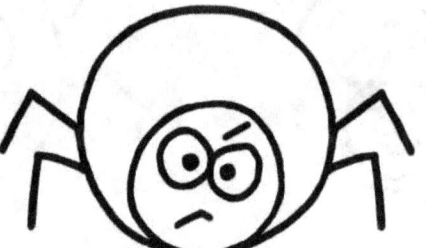

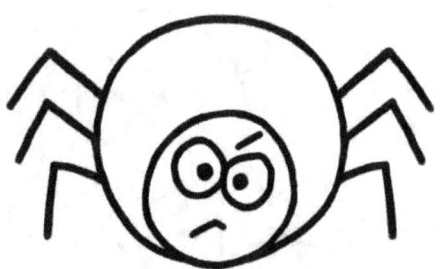 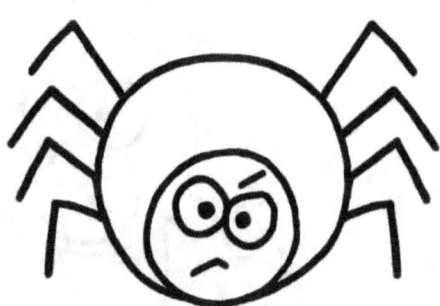

chick

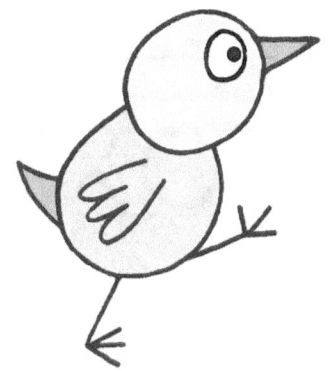

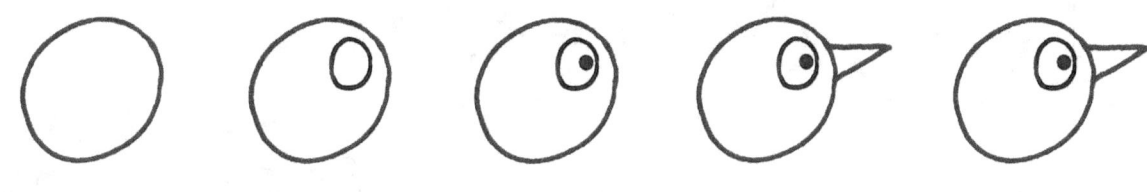

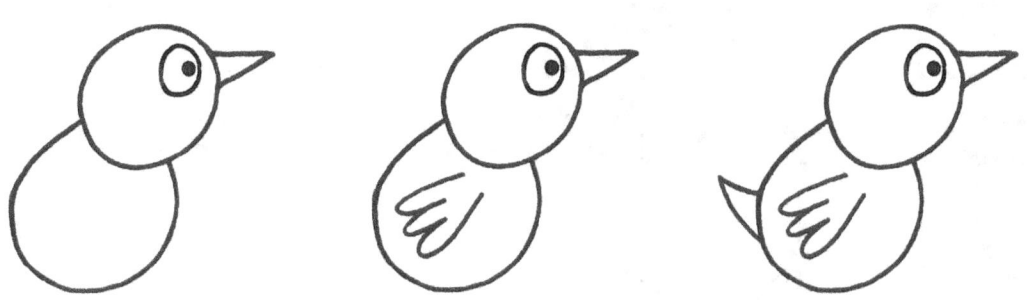

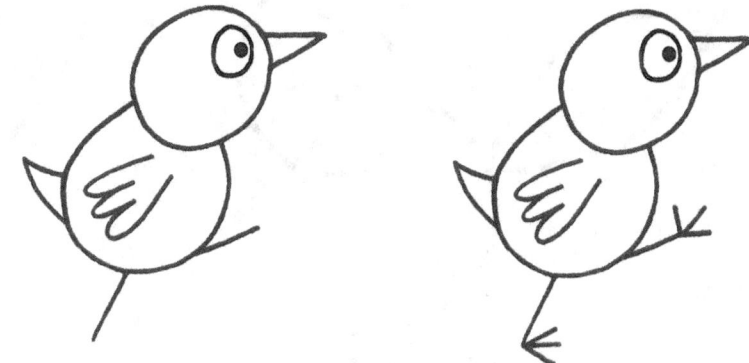

fox

pig

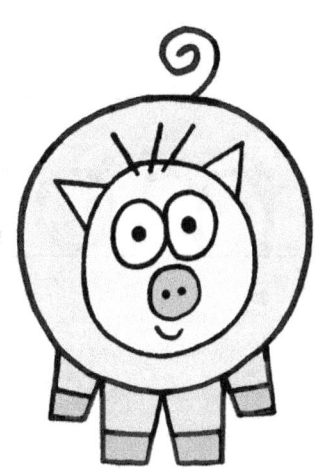

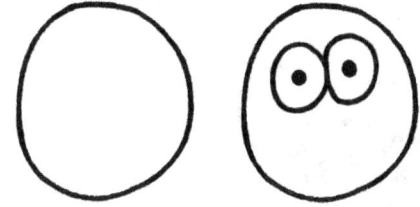

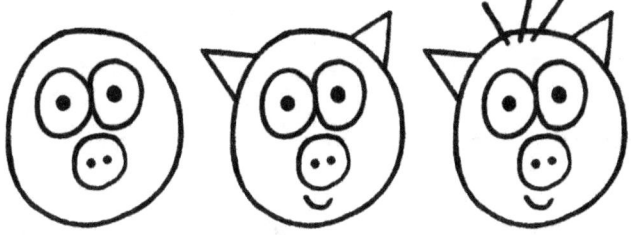

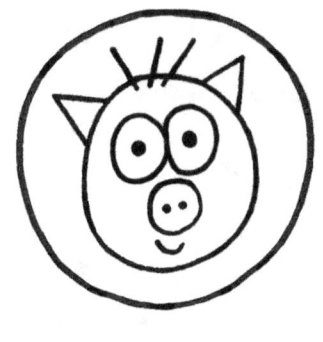 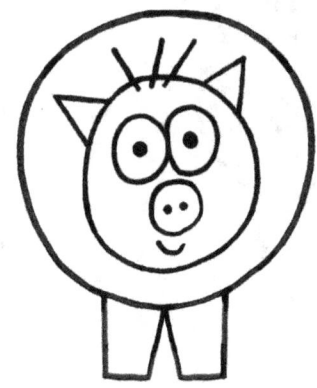 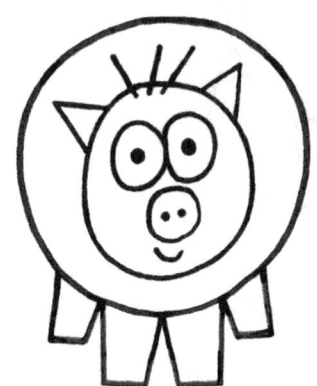

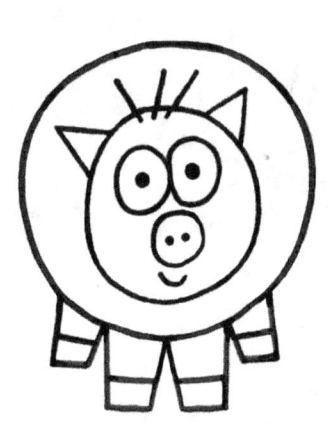 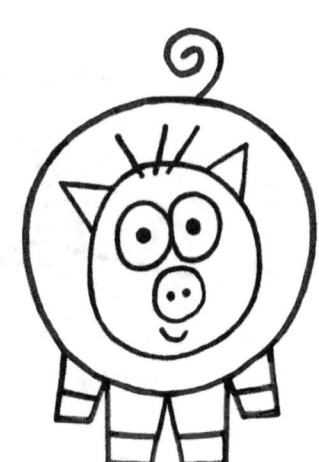

33

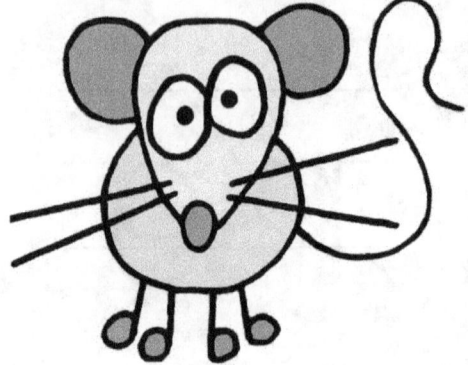

mouse

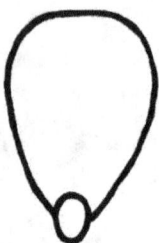 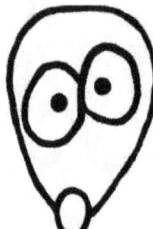 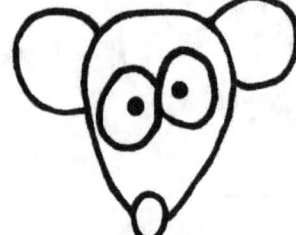

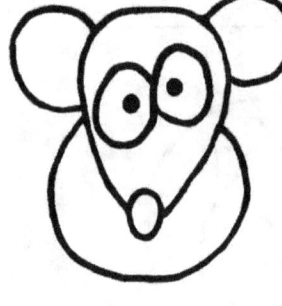 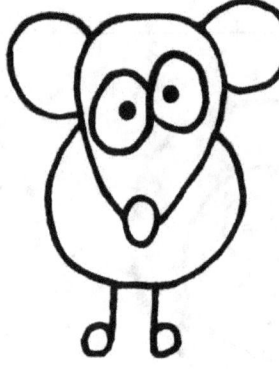 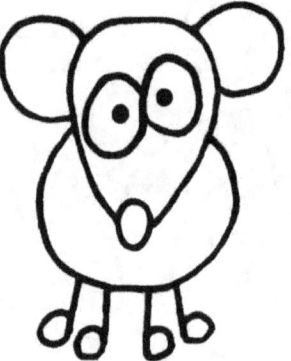

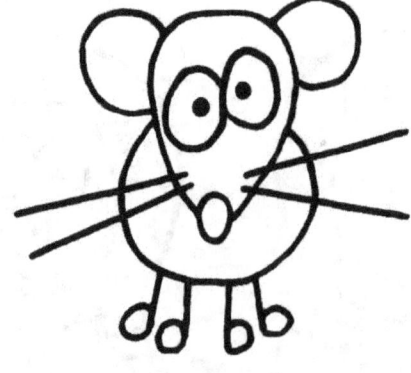 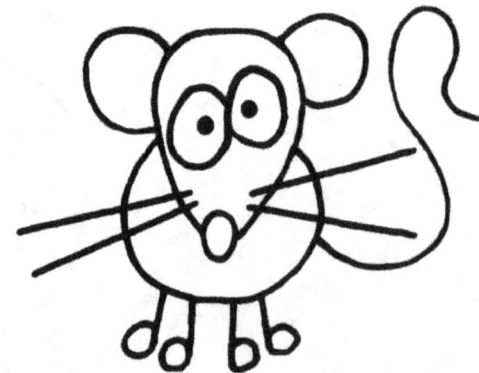

fish

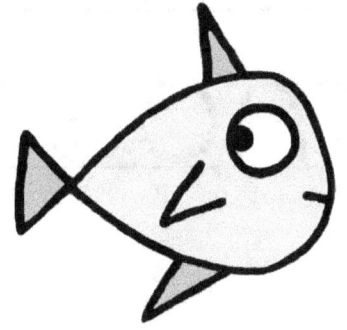

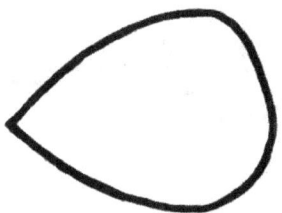 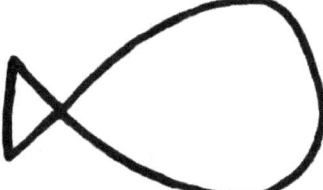

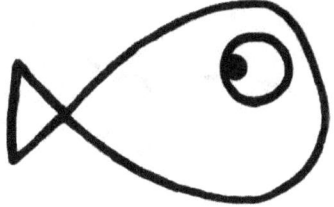 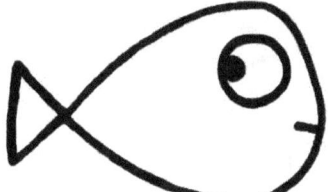

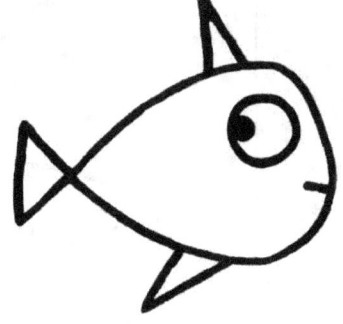 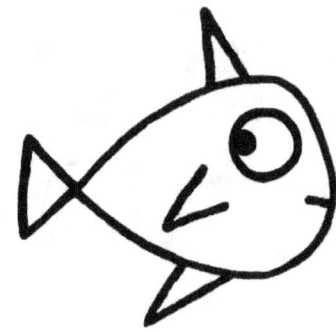

mosquito

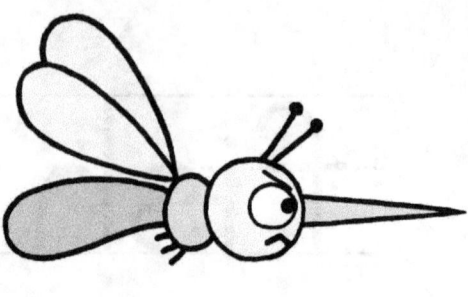

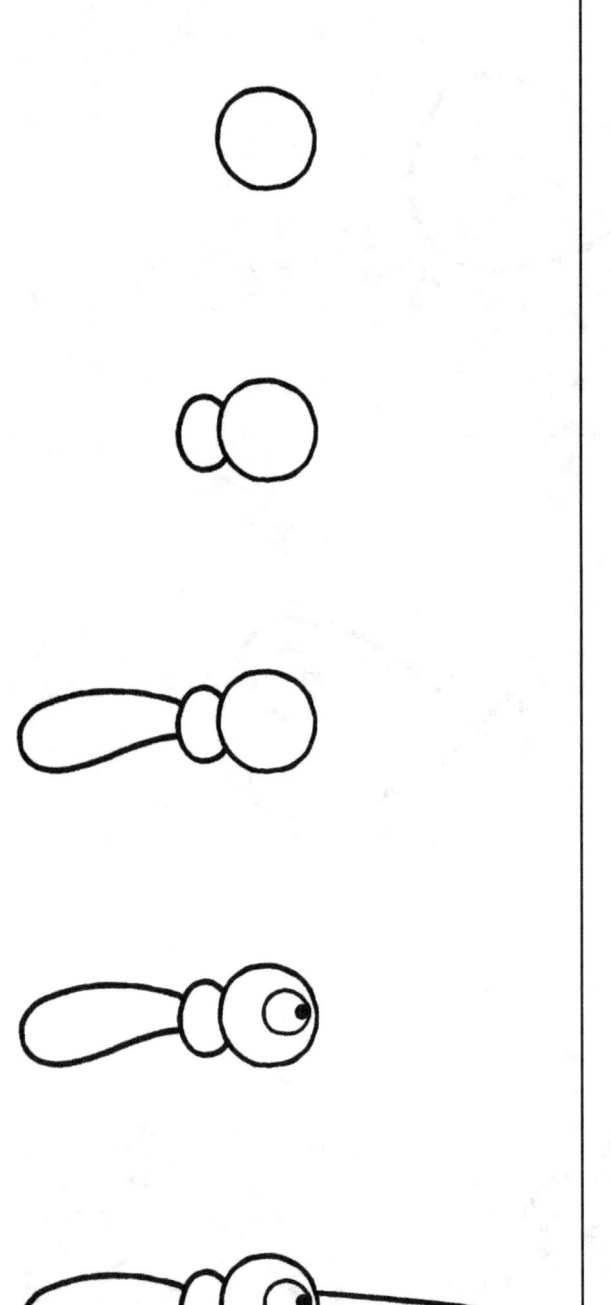

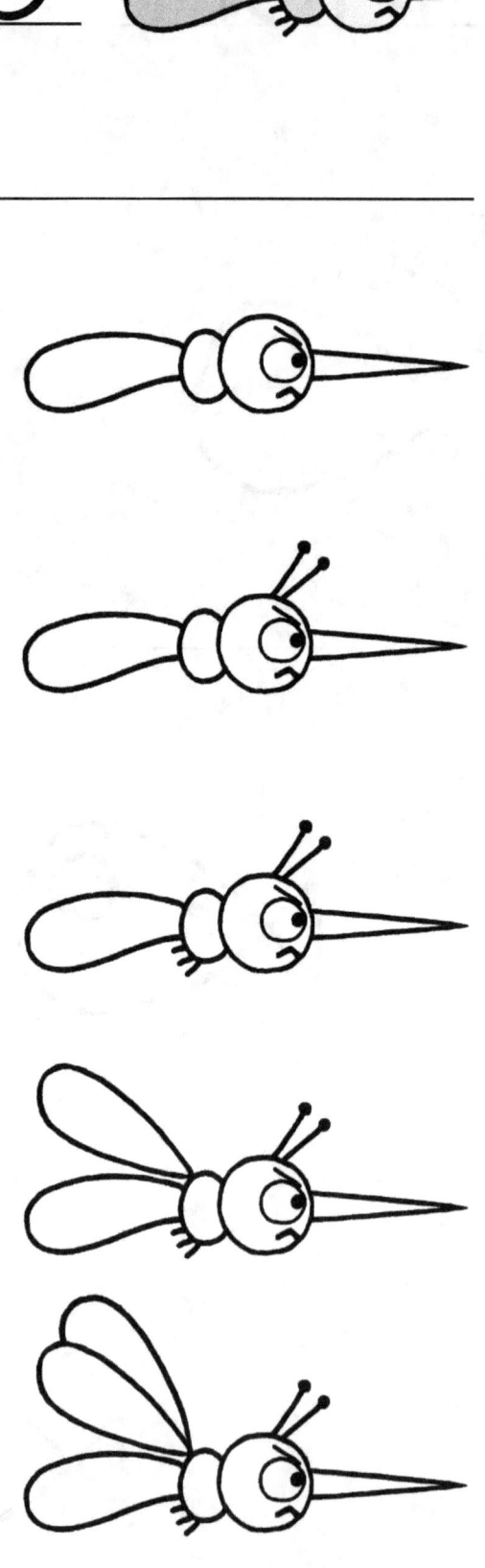

crab

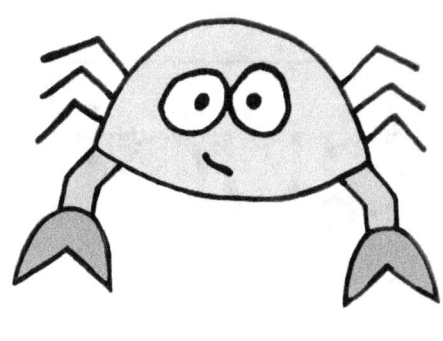

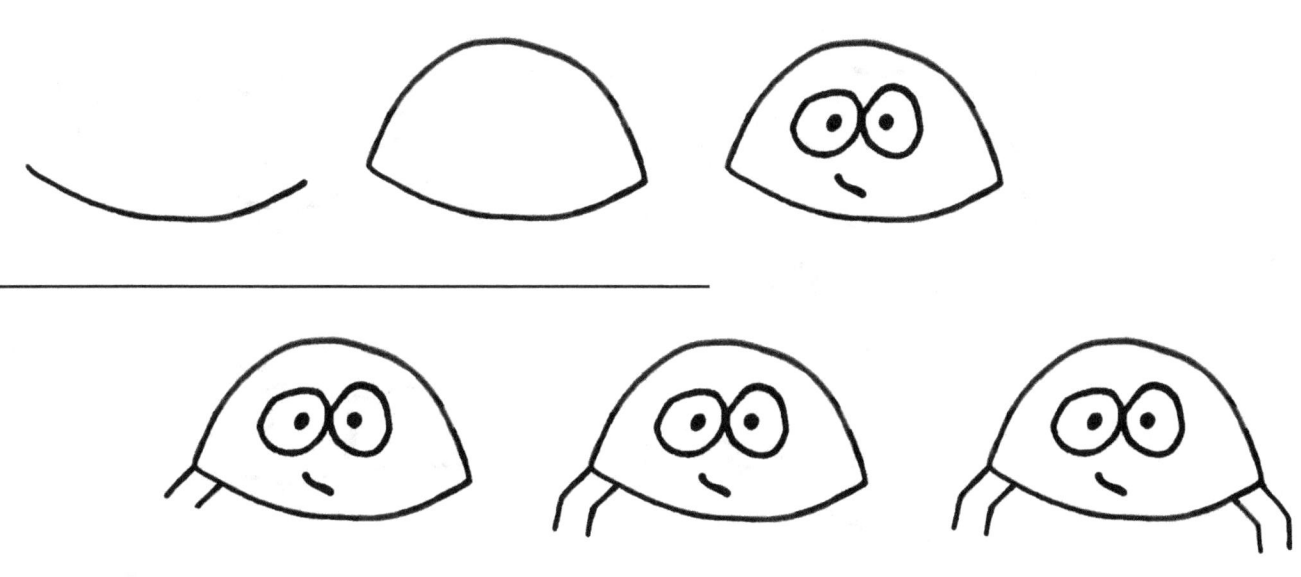

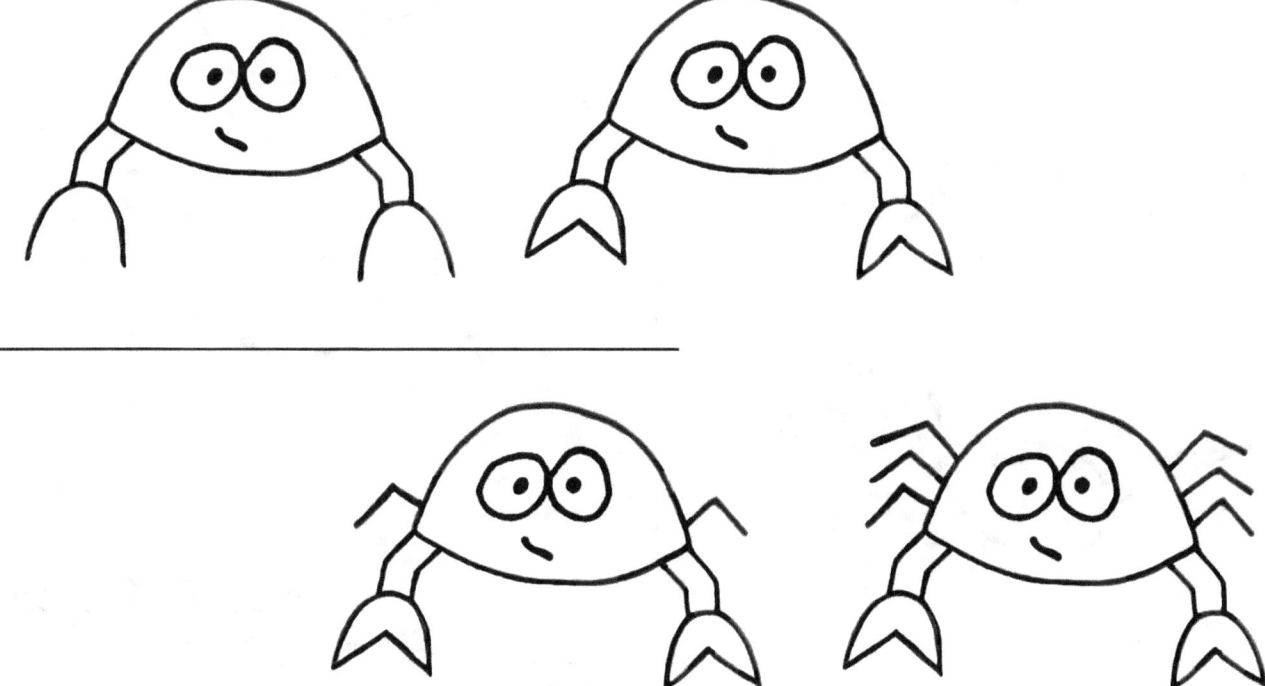

quail

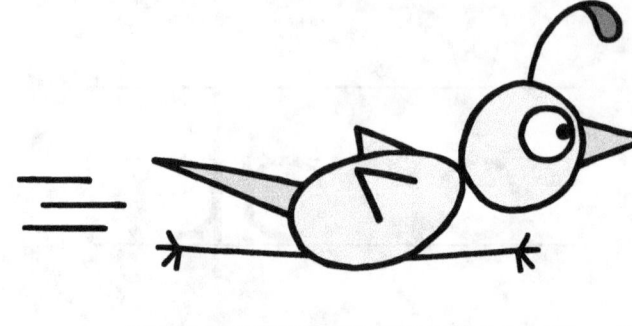

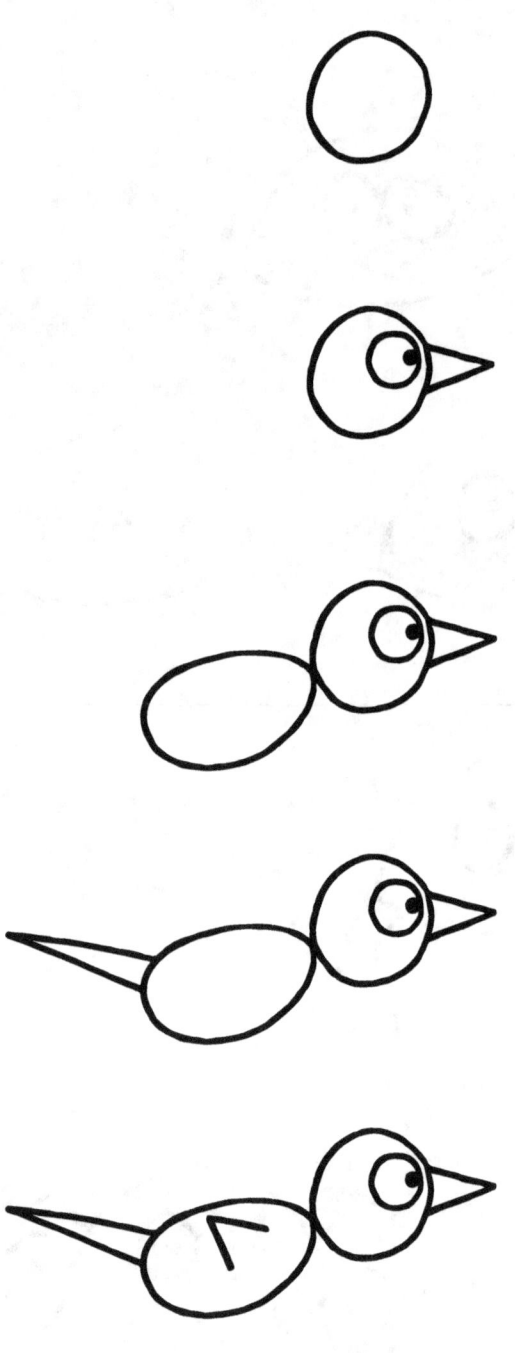

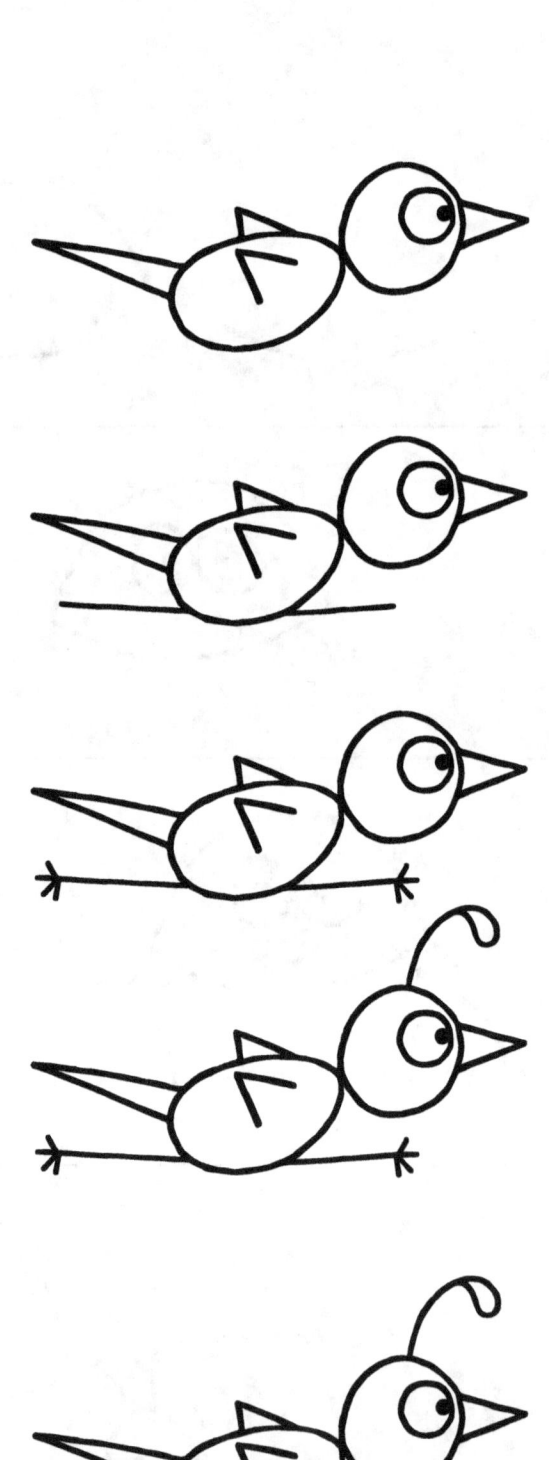

caterpillar

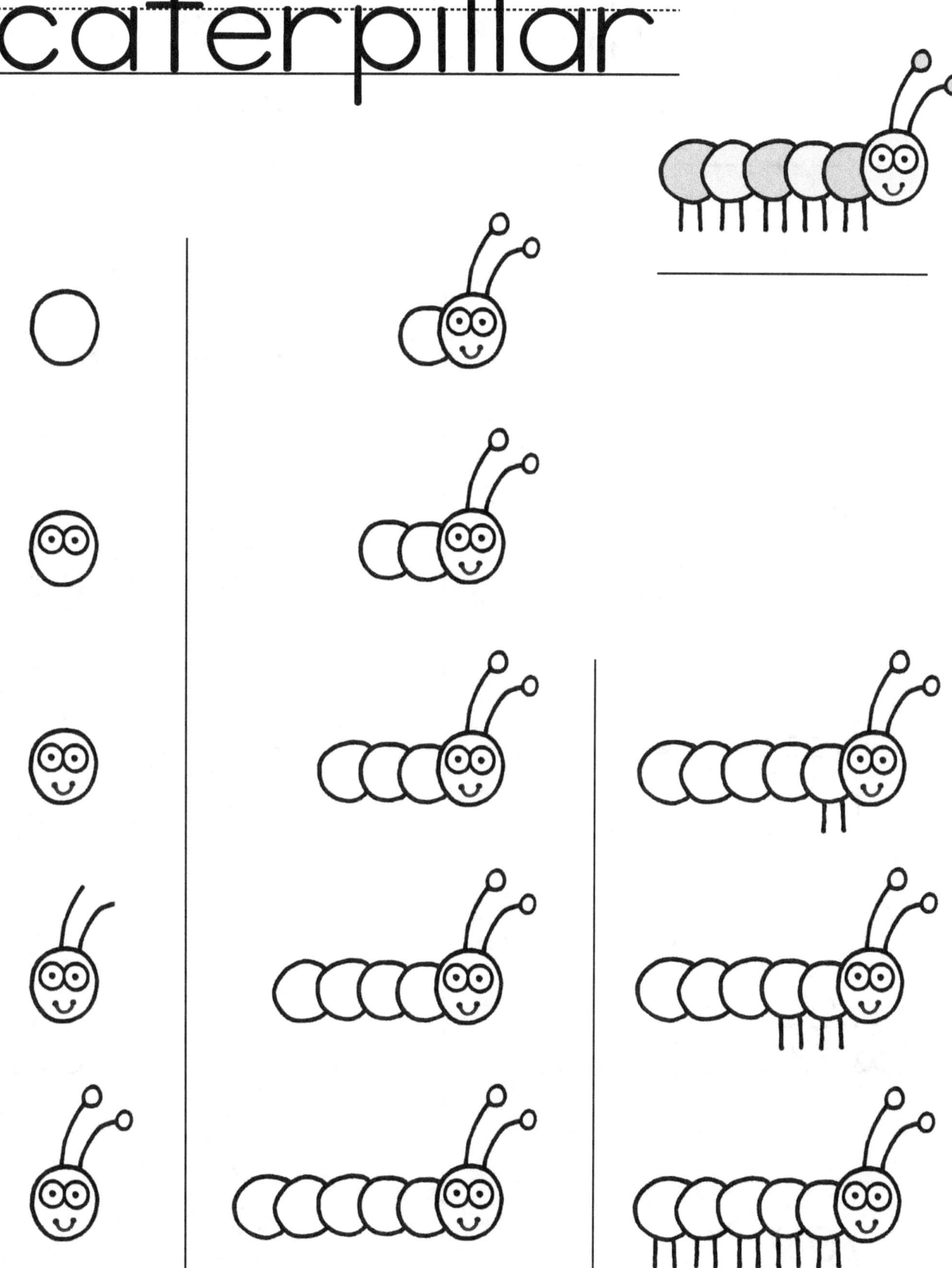

whale

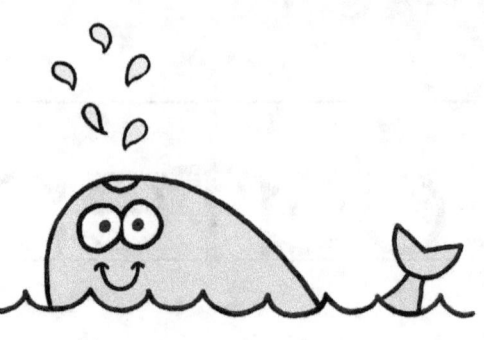

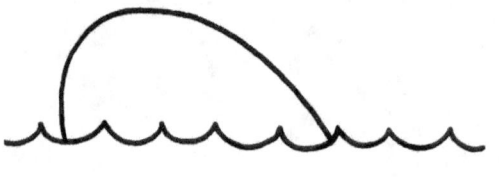

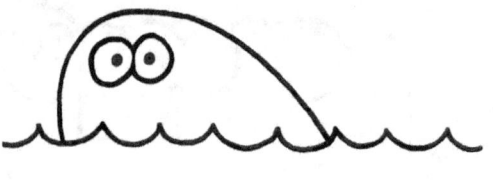

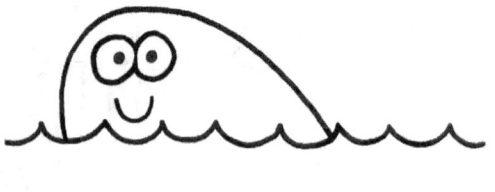

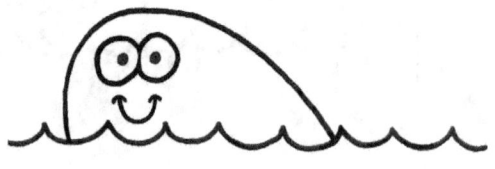

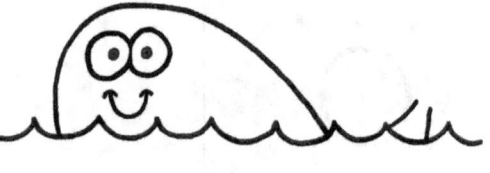

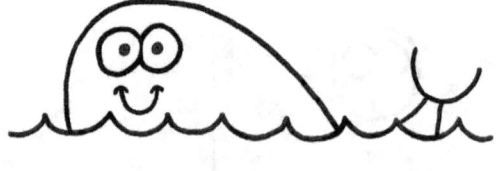

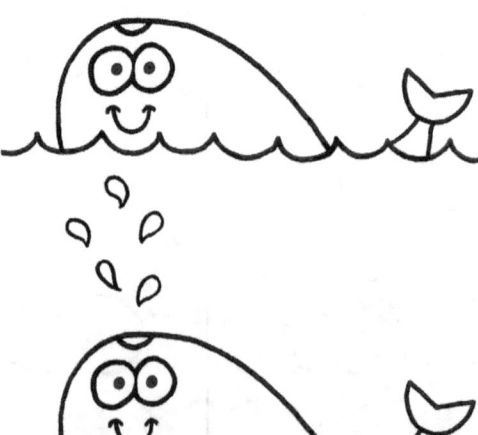

shark

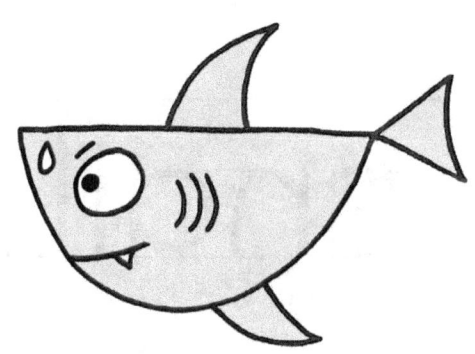

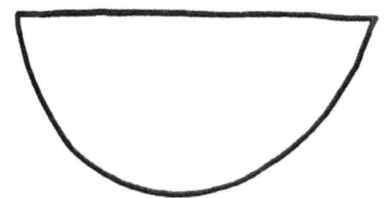 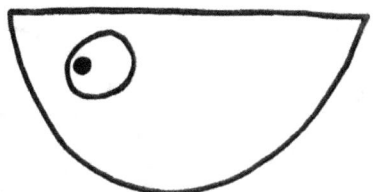

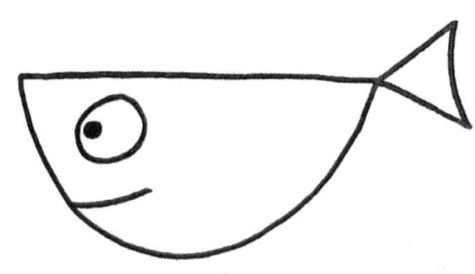 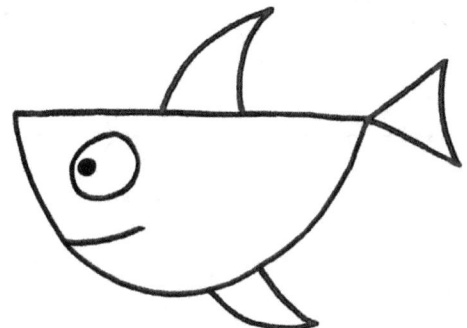

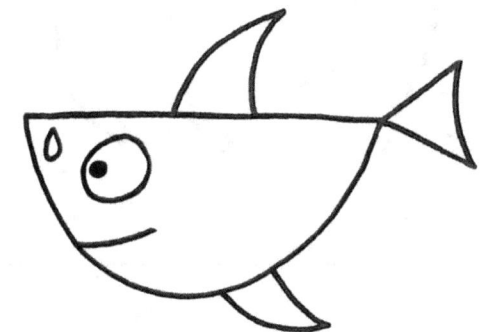 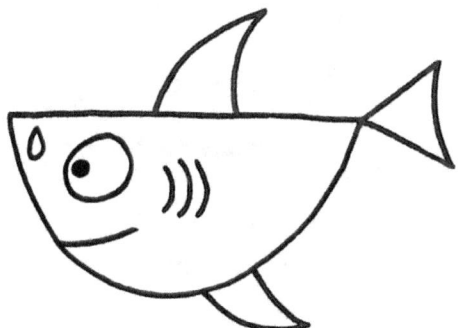

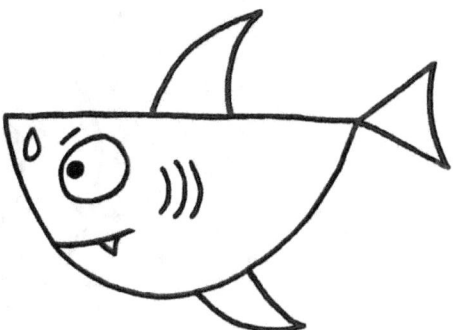

snail

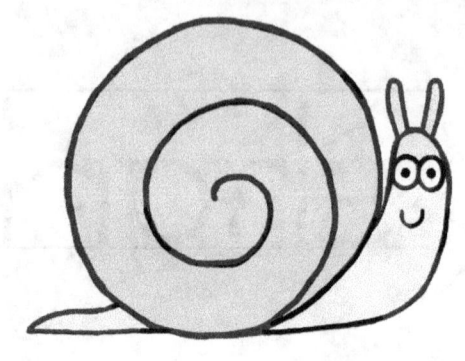

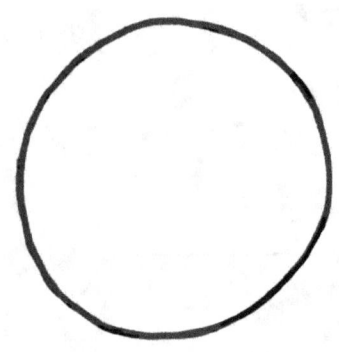
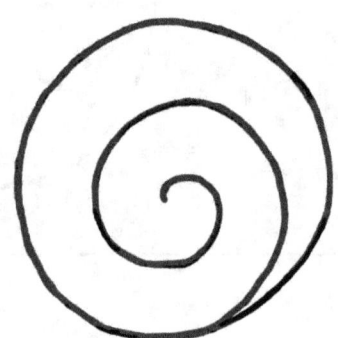

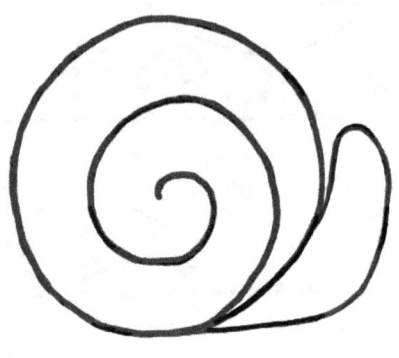
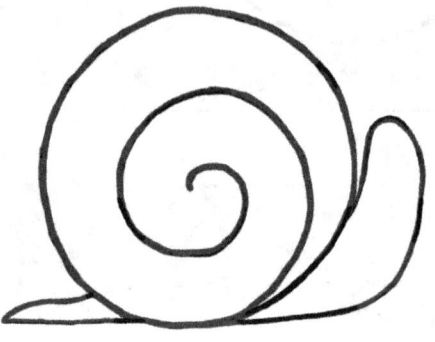

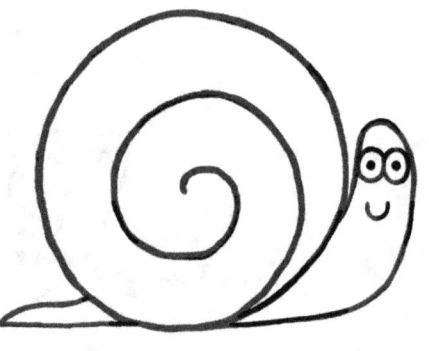
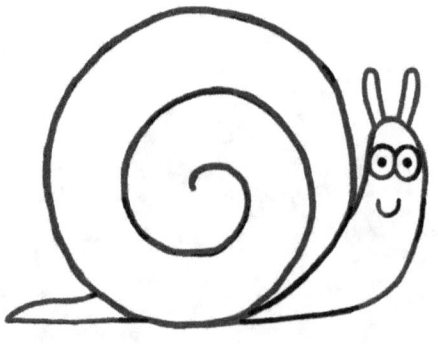

squirrel

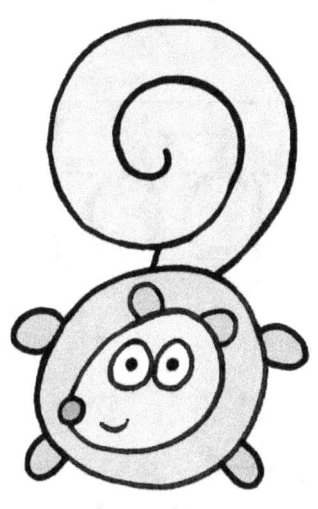

_____

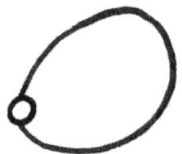 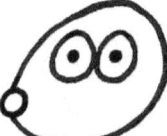 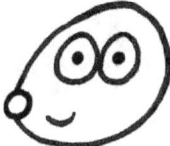 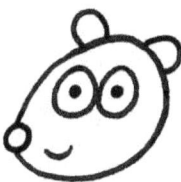

_____

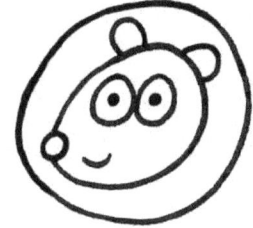 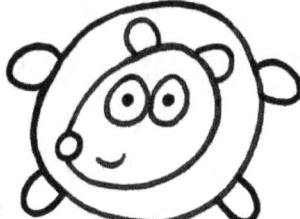

_____

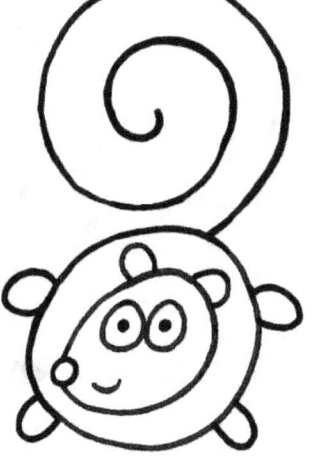 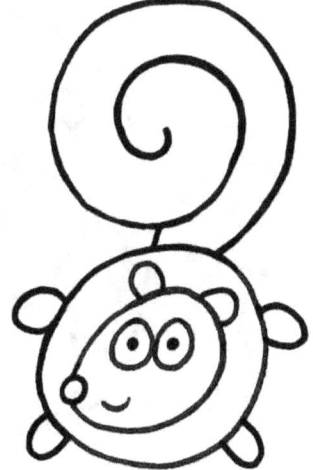

polar bear

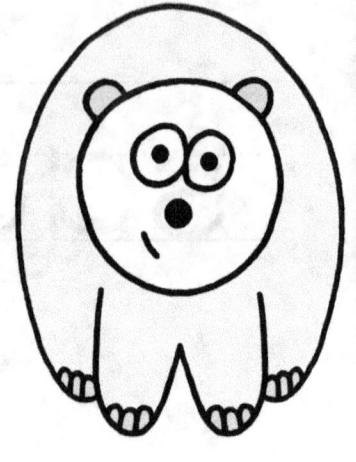

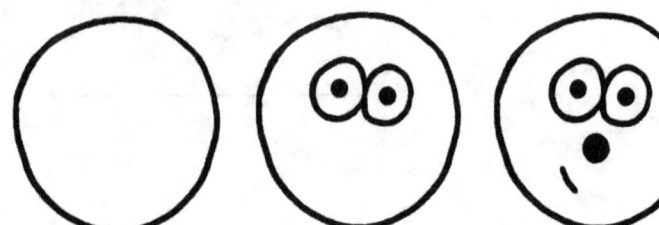

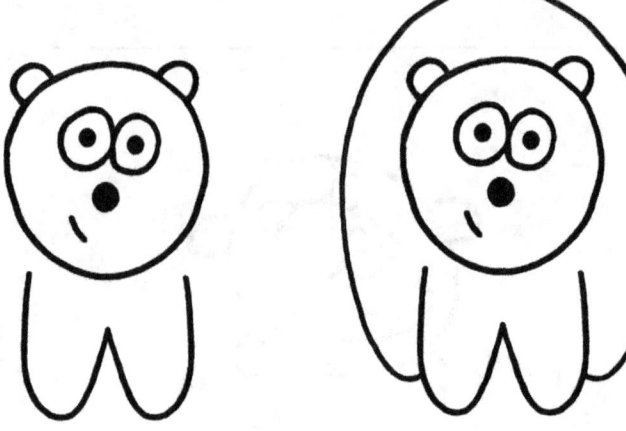

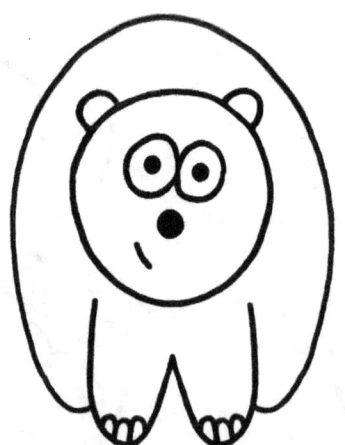

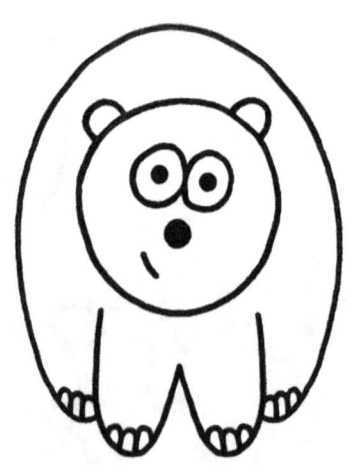

penguin

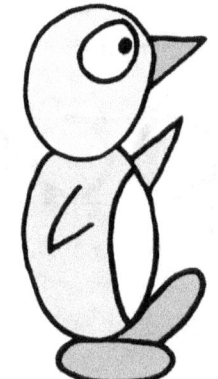

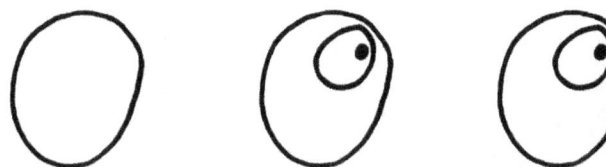

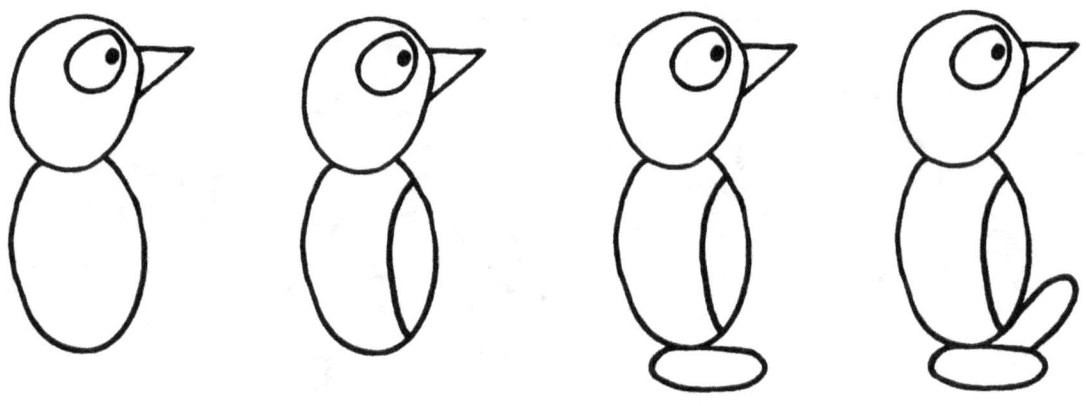

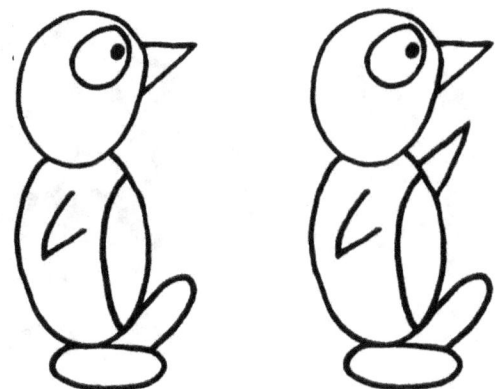

poodle

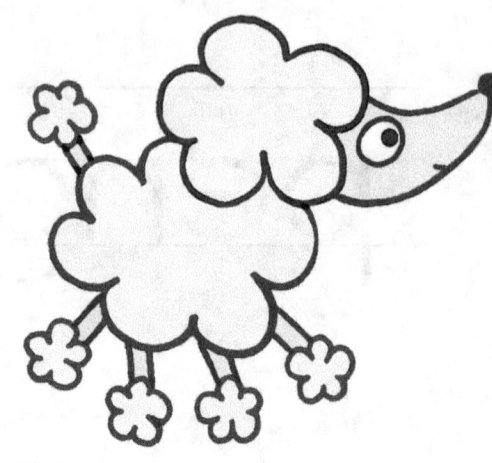

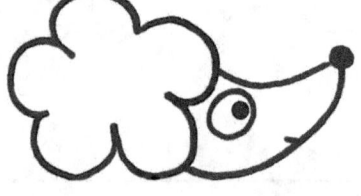

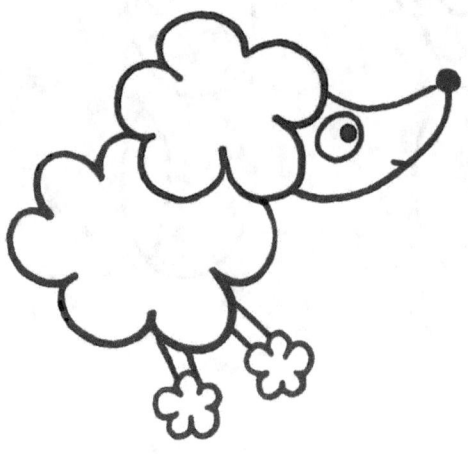

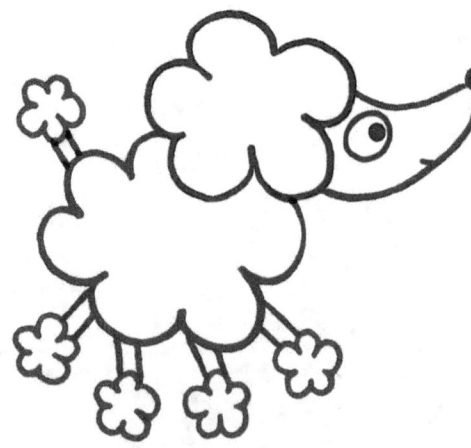

sheep

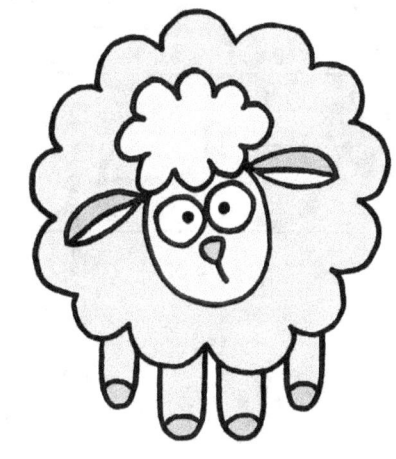

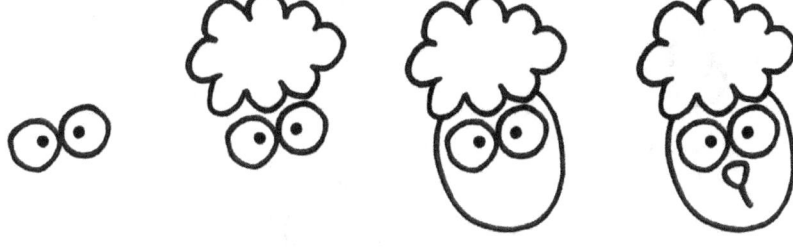

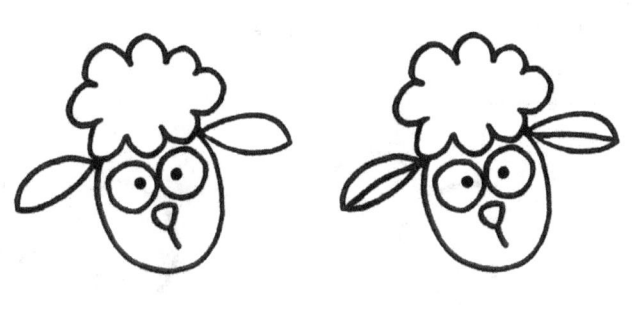
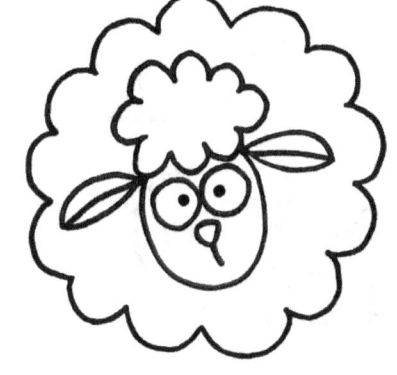

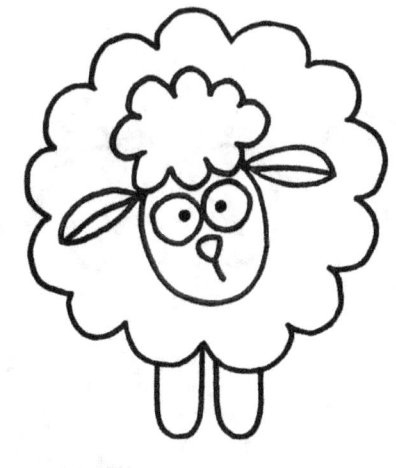
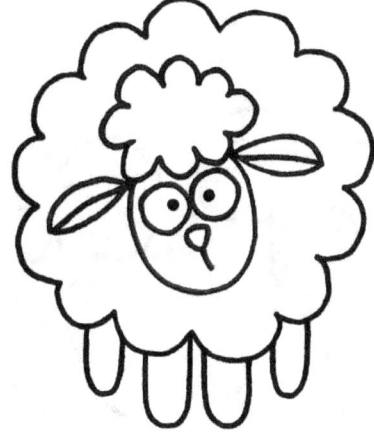
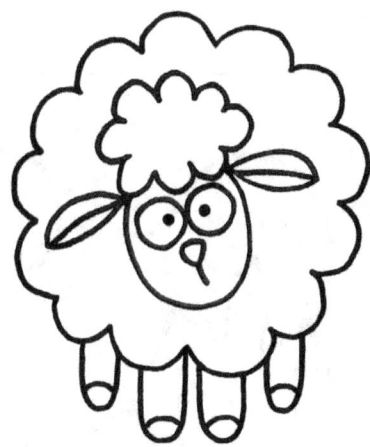

elephant

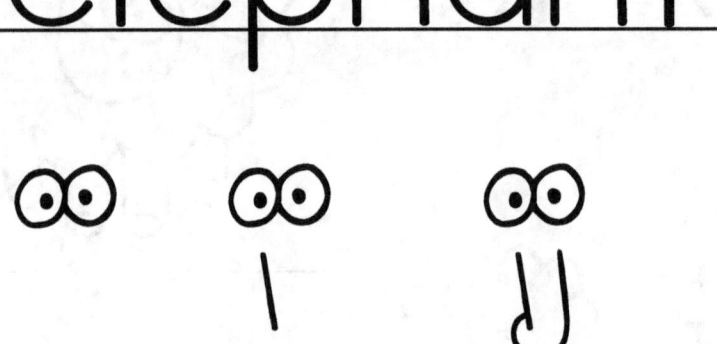
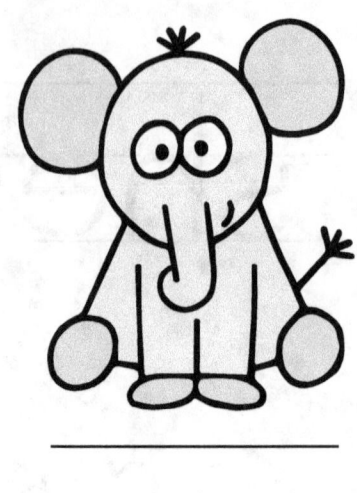

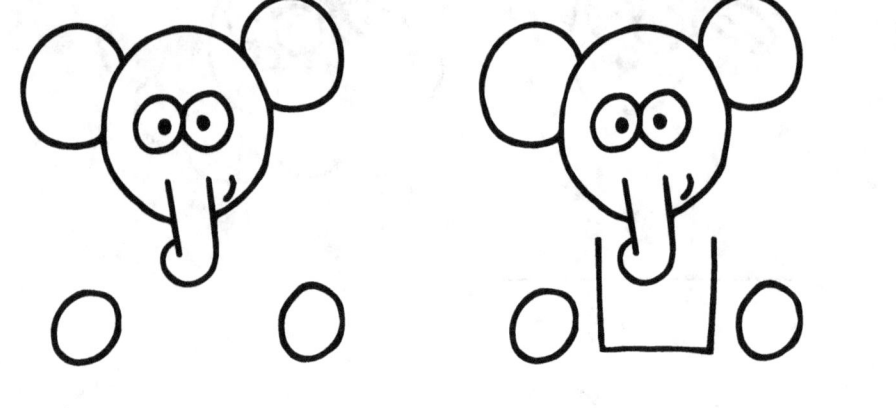
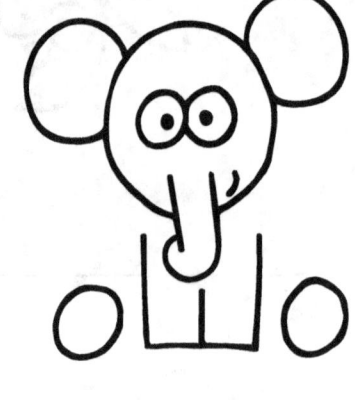

umbrella bird

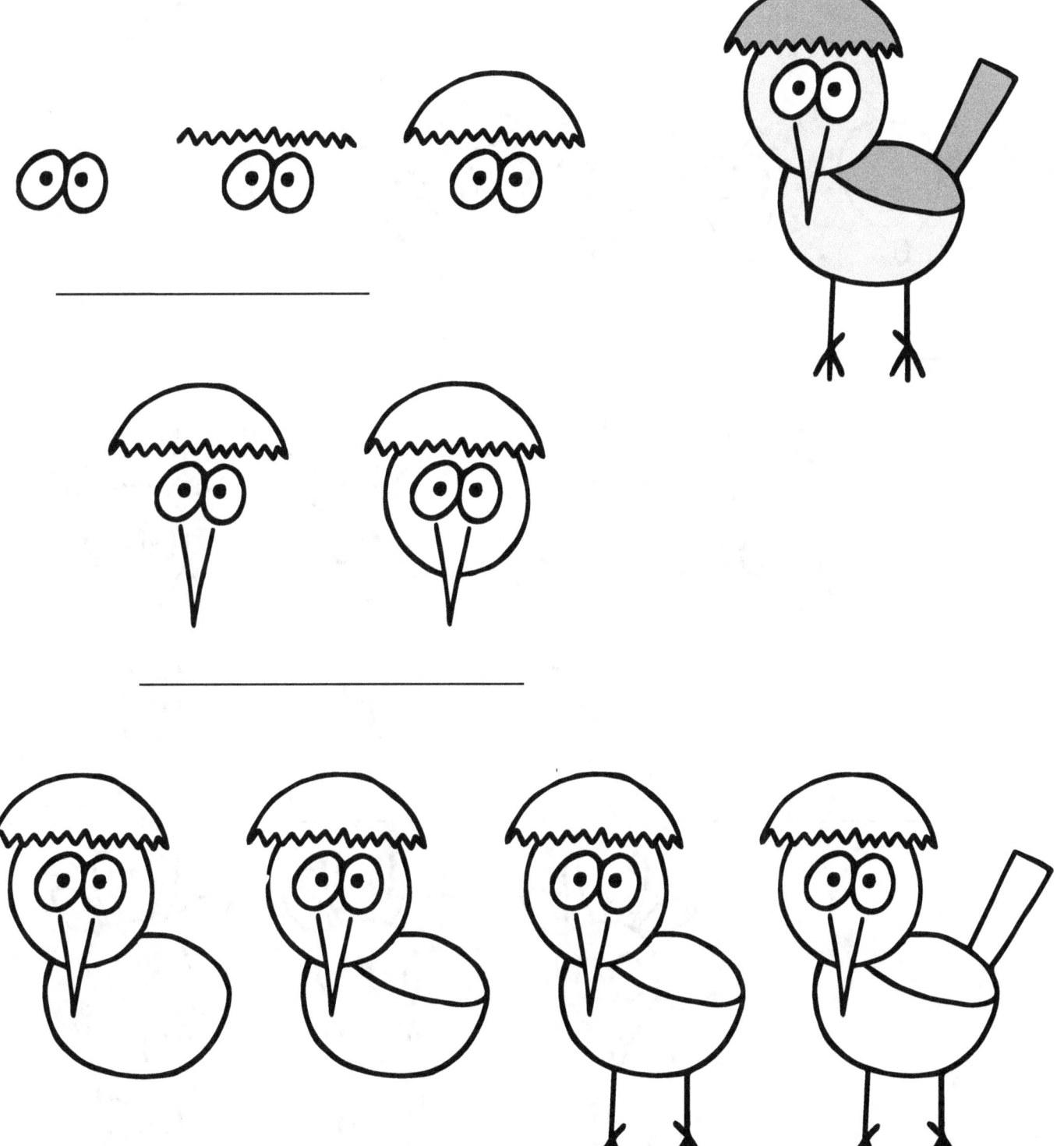

deer

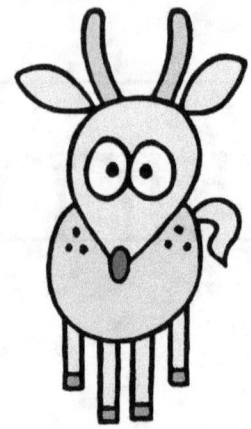

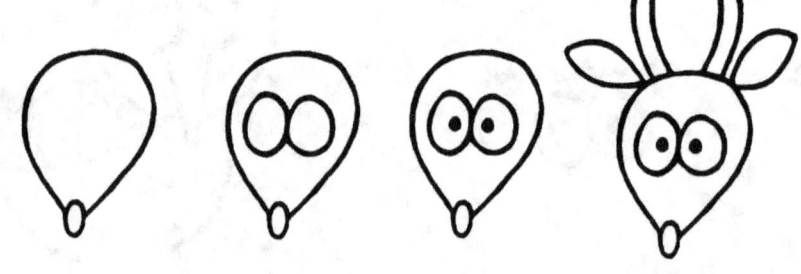

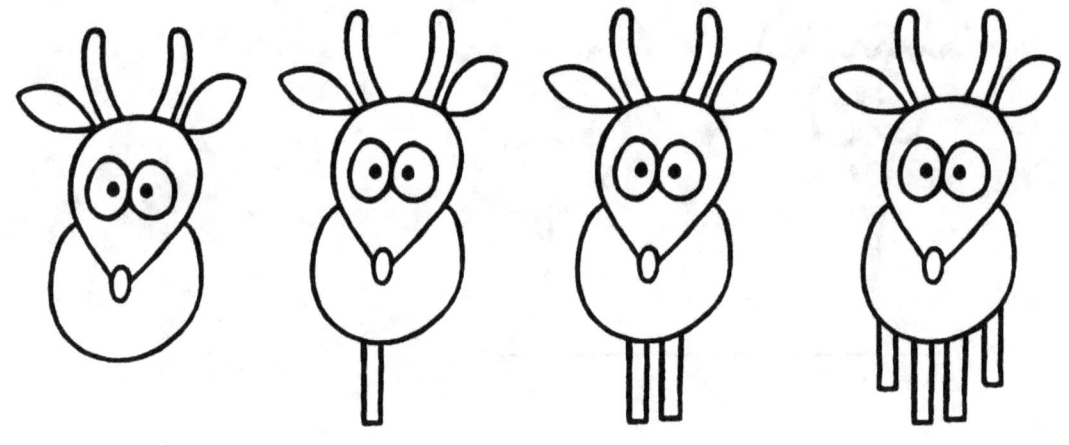

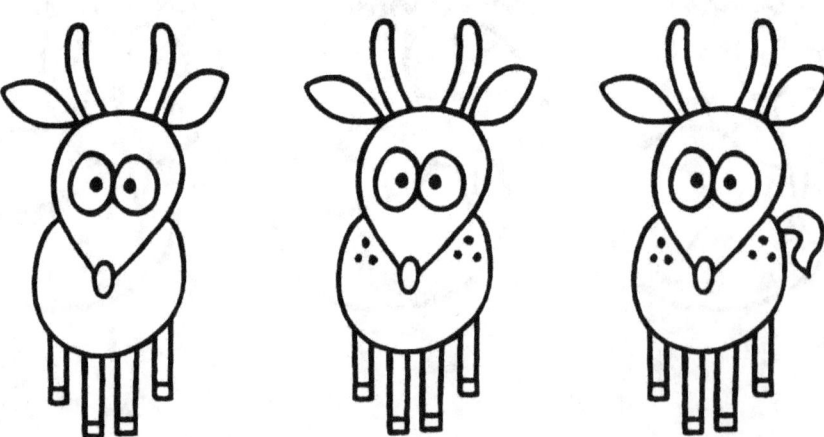

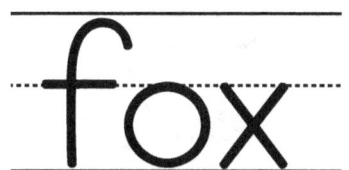 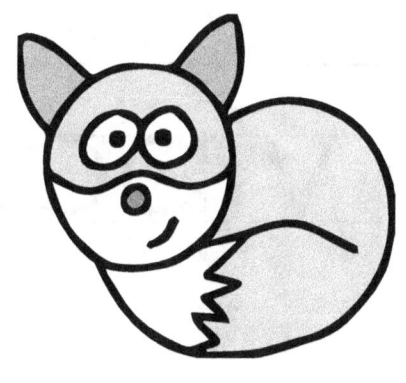

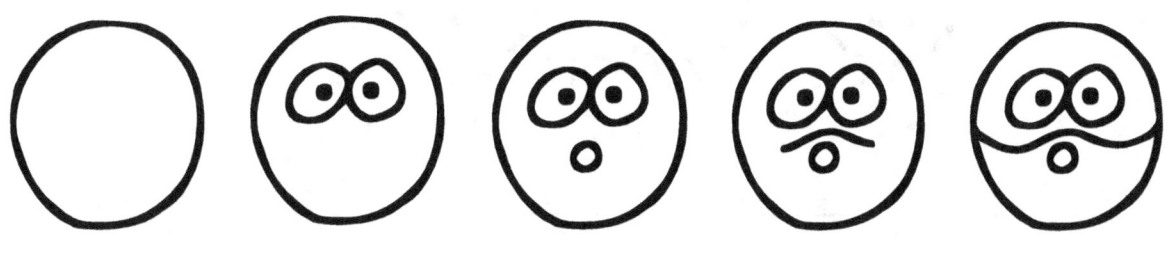

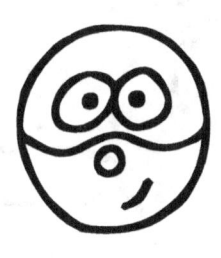 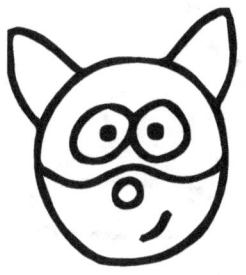 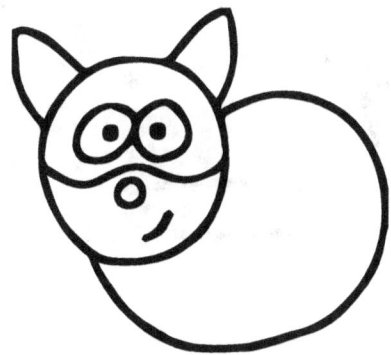

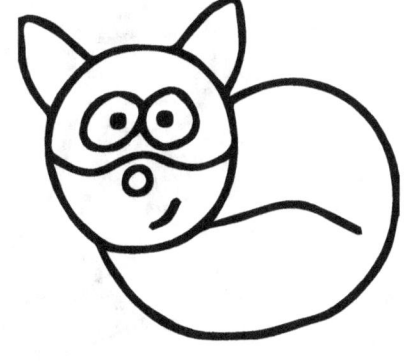 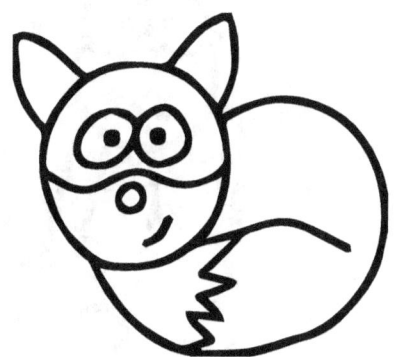

viper

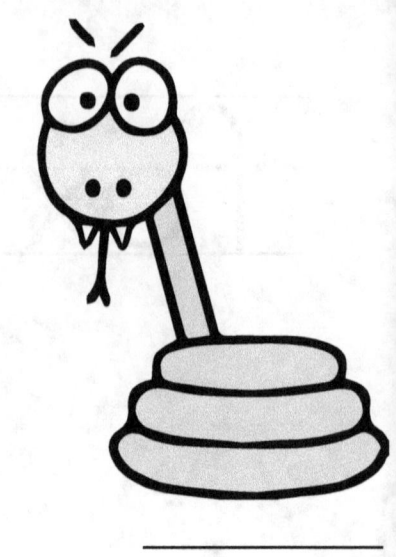

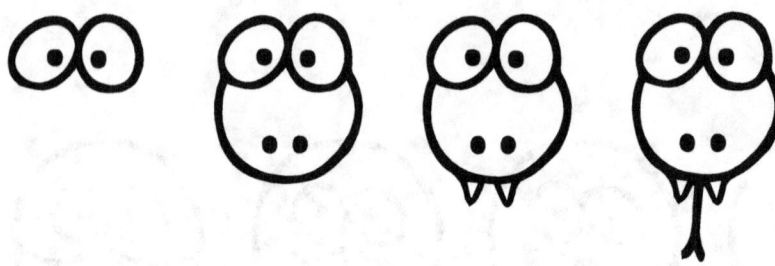

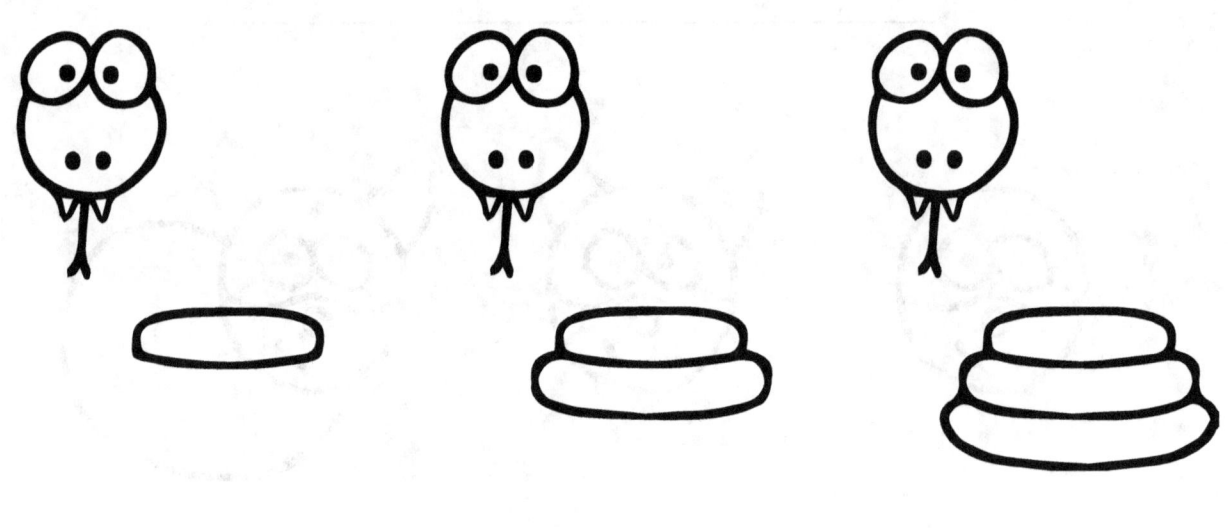

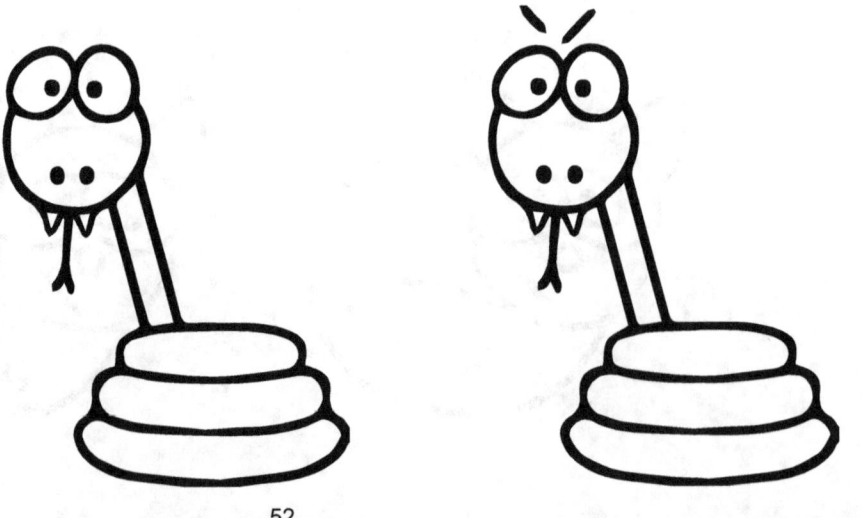

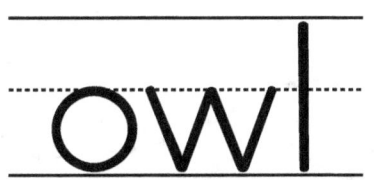 owl

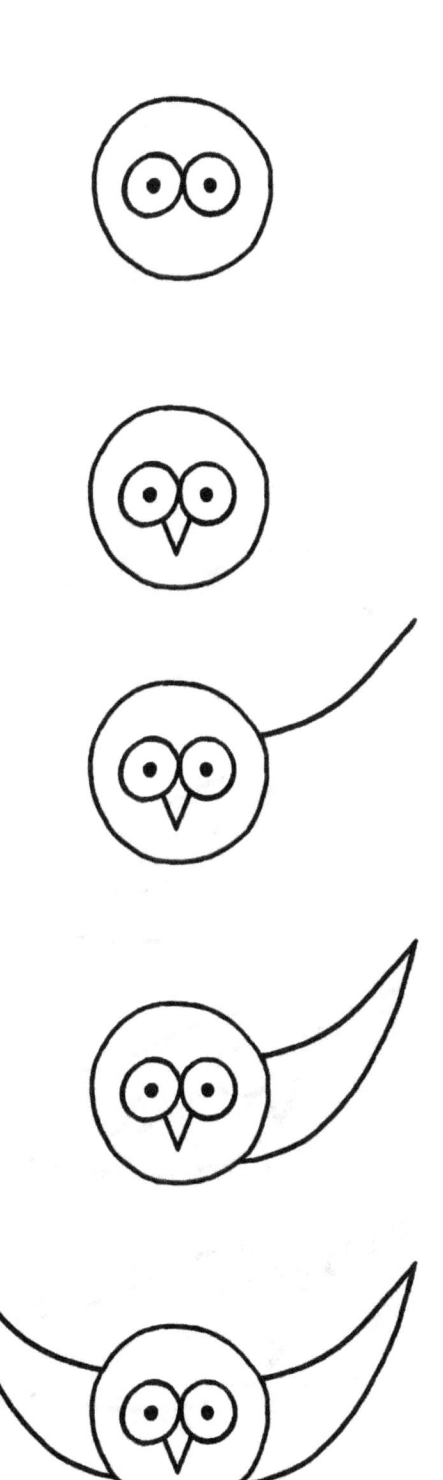

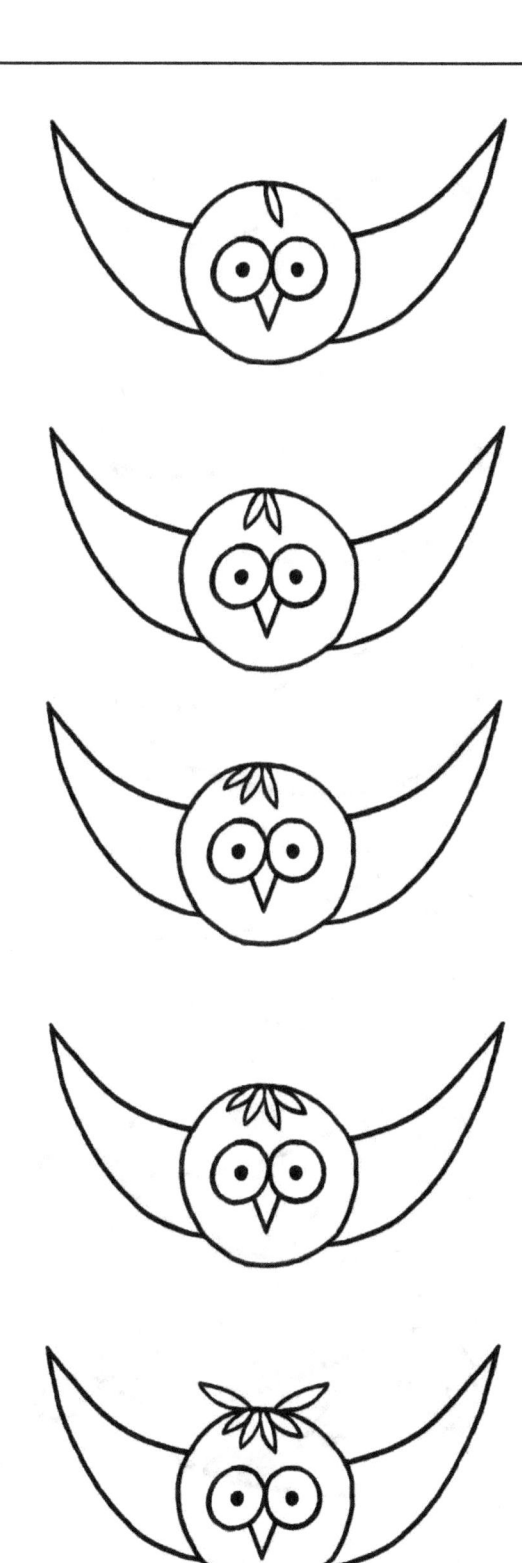

narwal

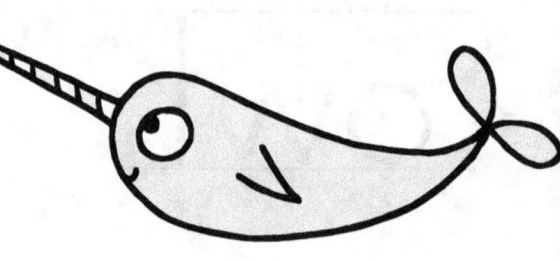

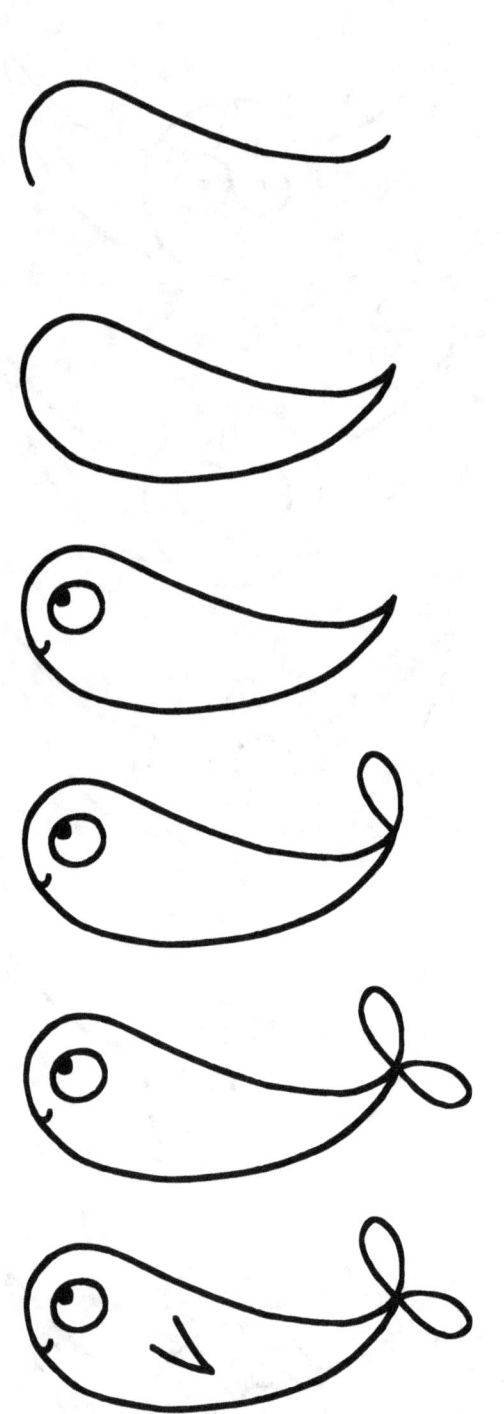

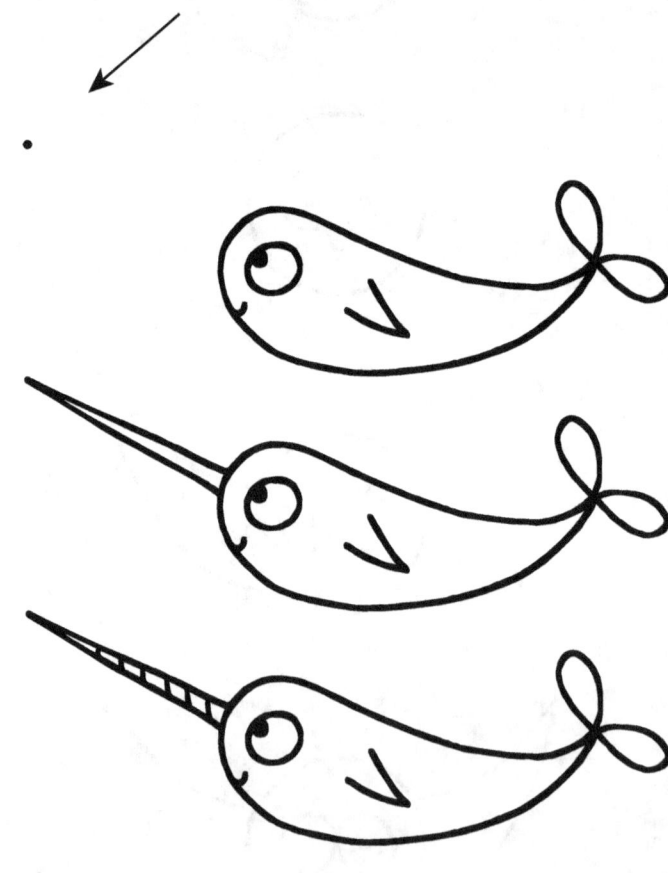

unicorn

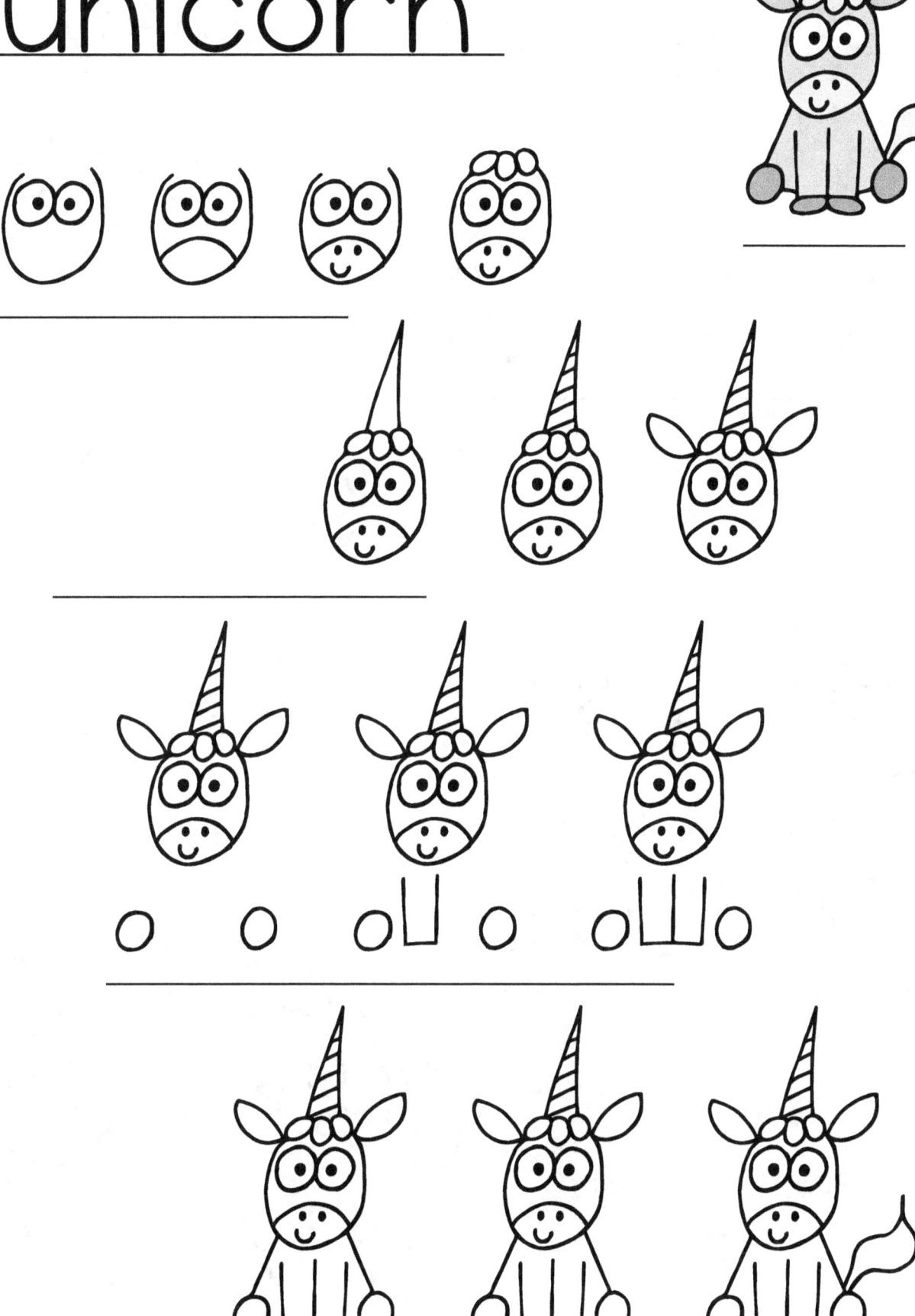

dog

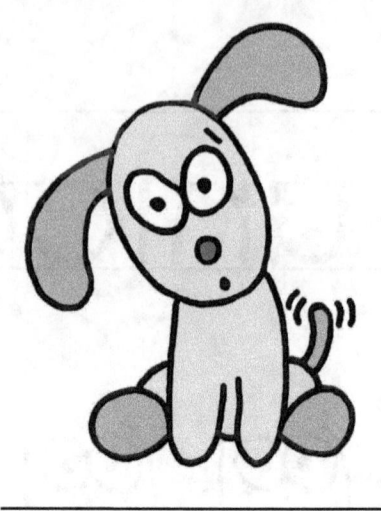

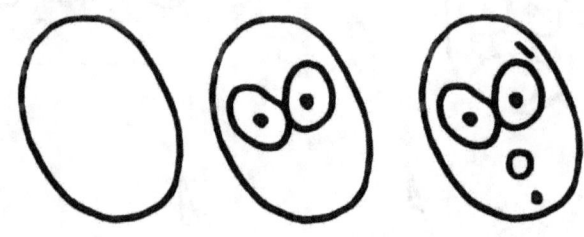

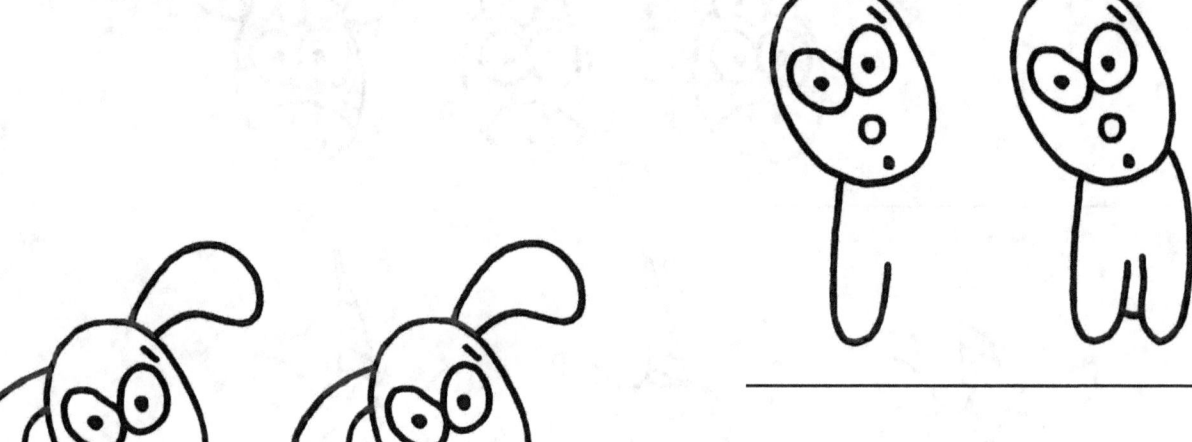

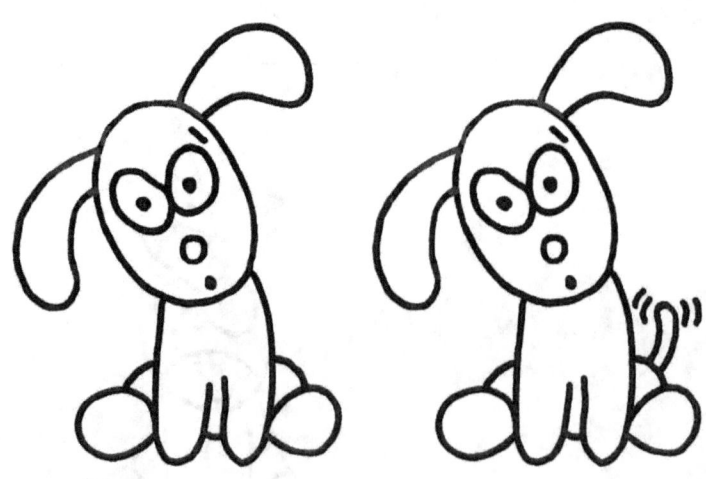

turtle

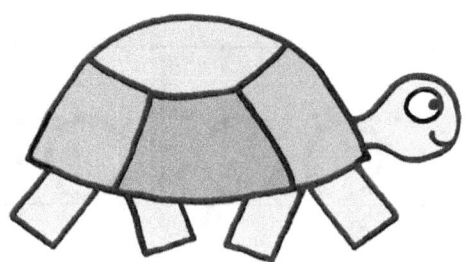

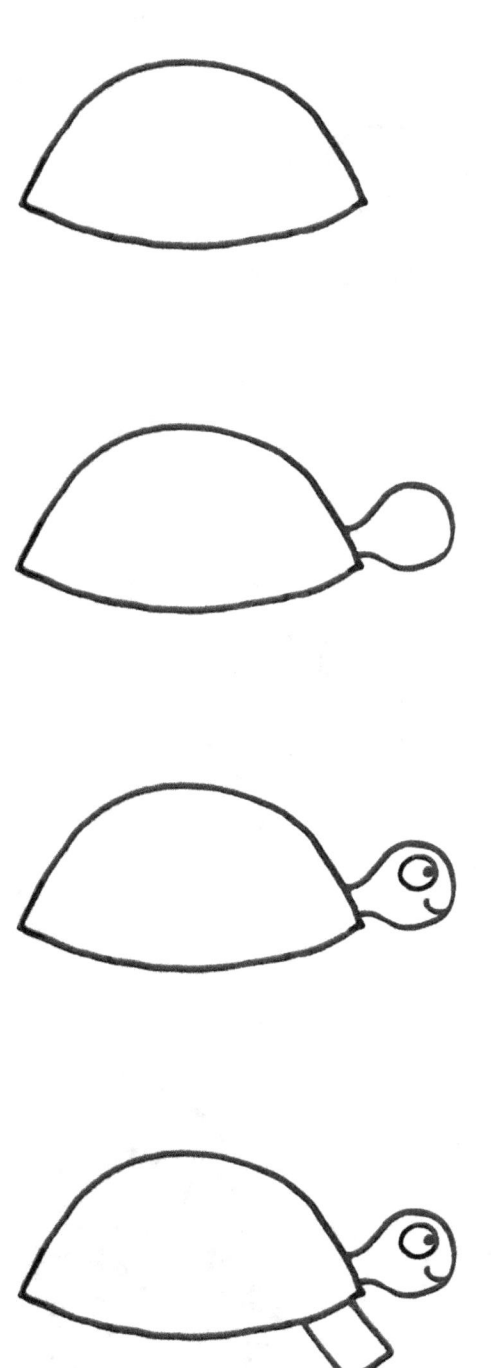

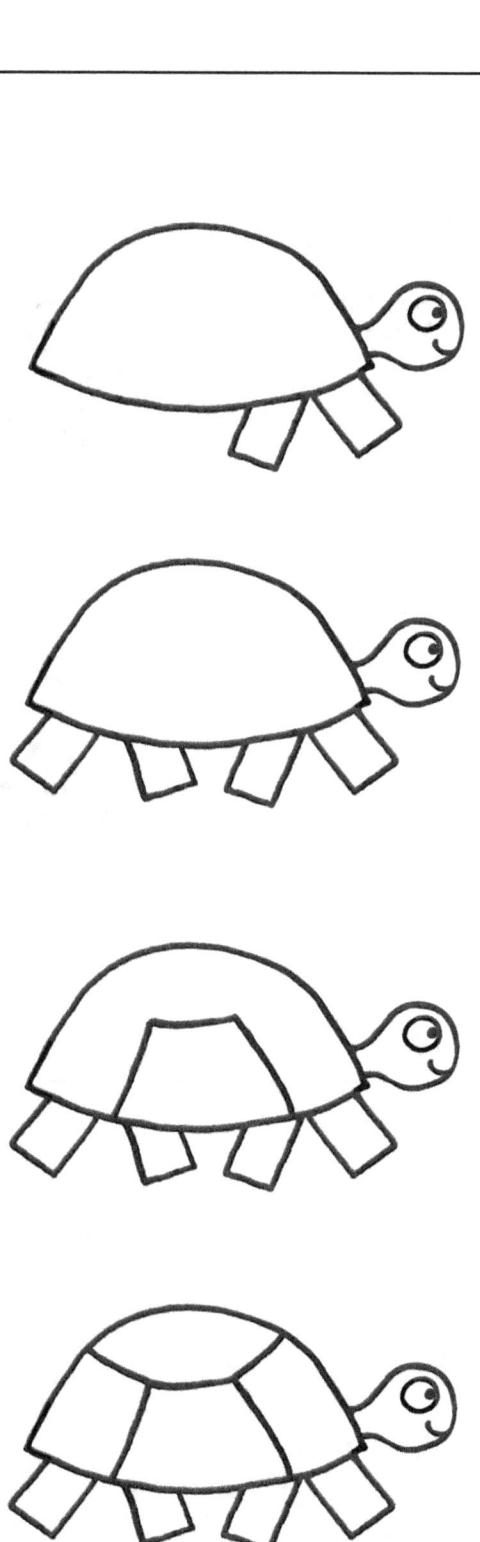

octopus

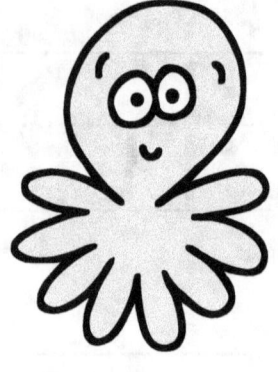

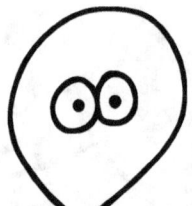 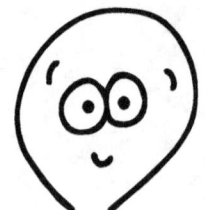

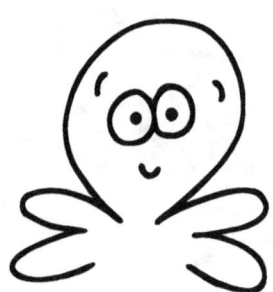

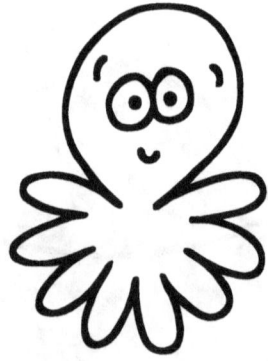

ladybug

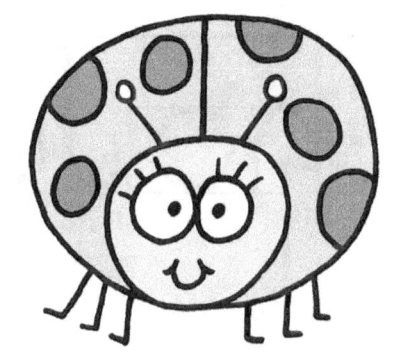

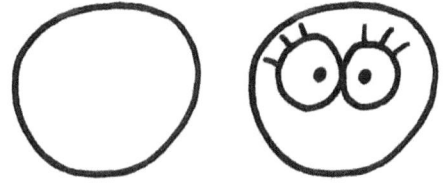

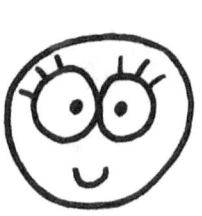 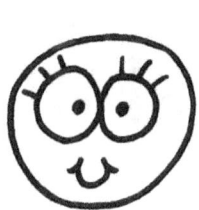 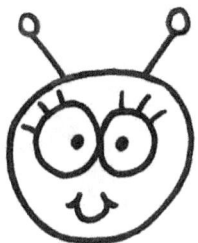

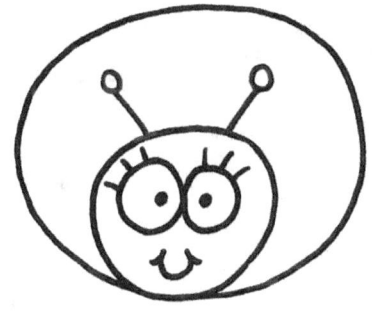 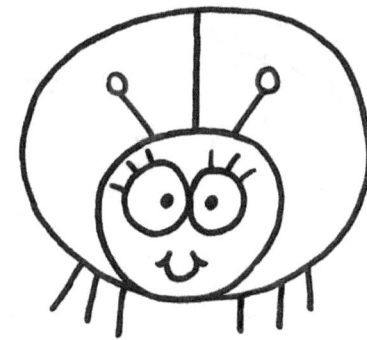 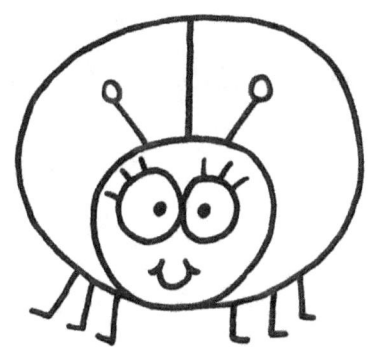

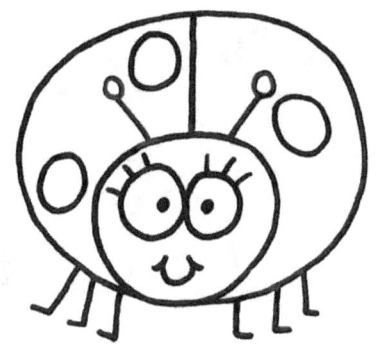 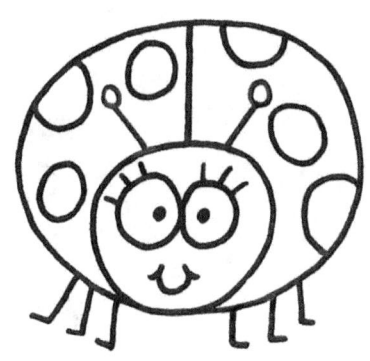

hedgehog

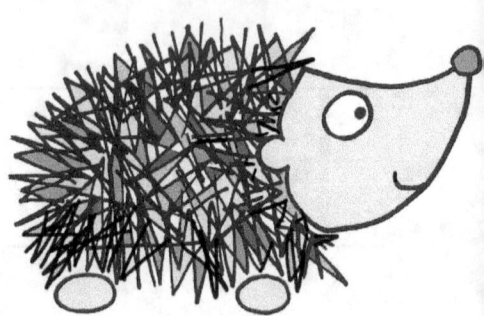

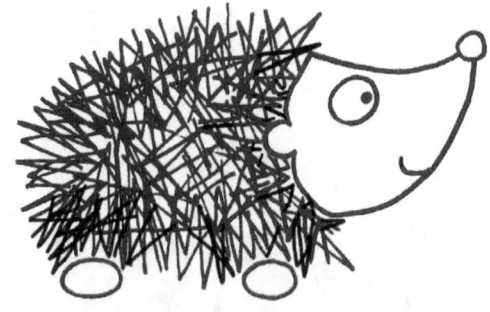

yak

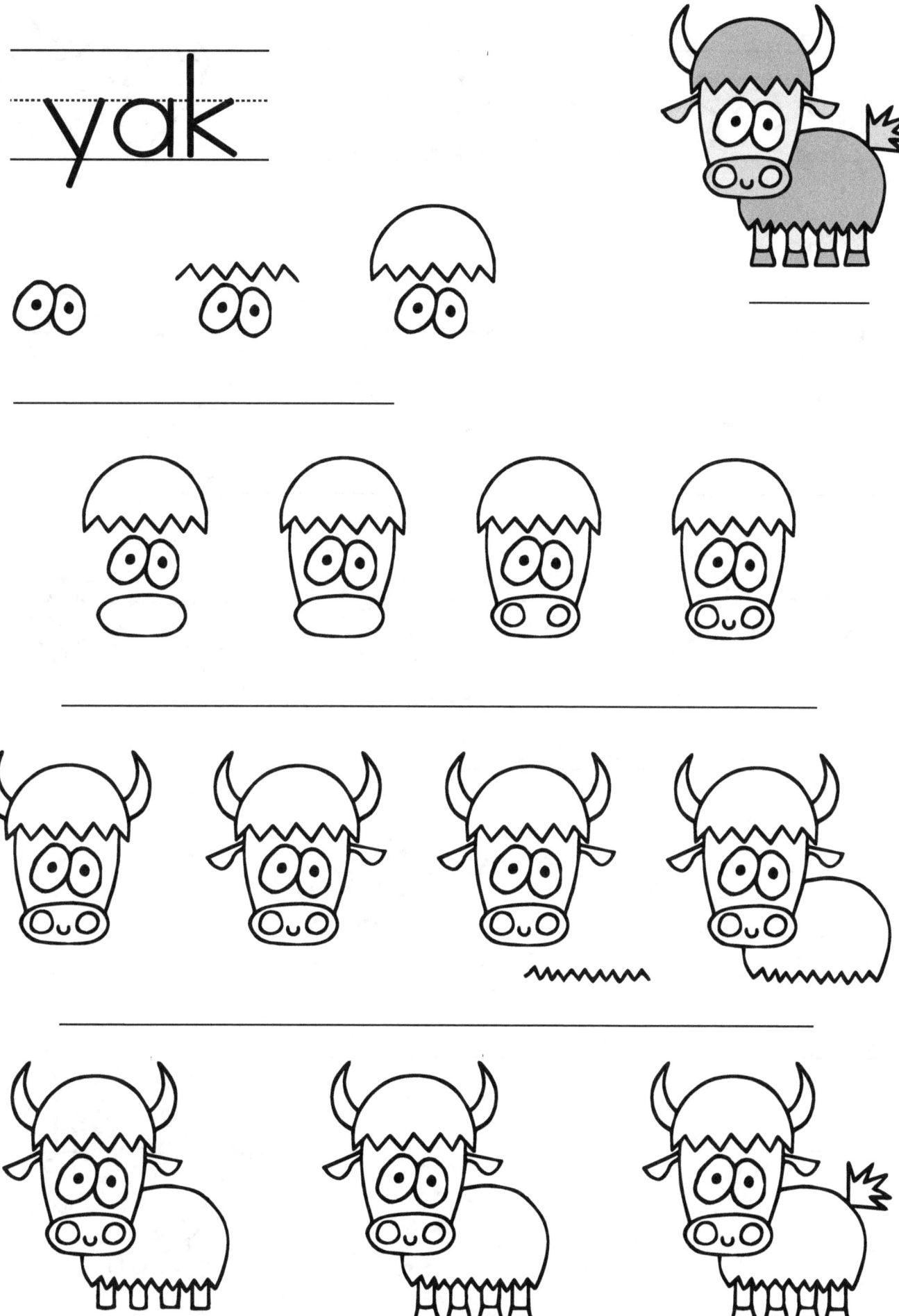

crocodile

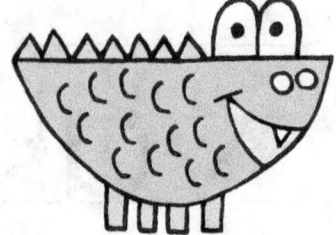

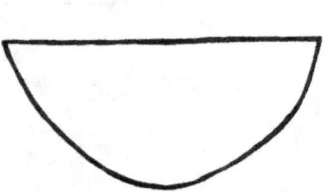
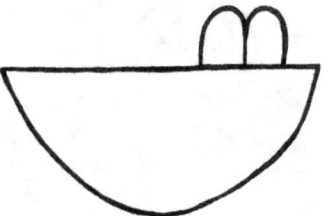
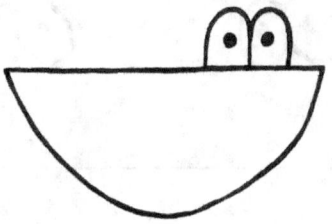

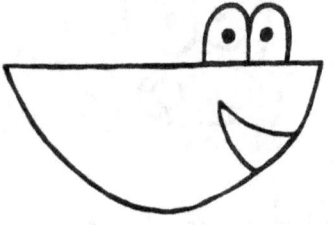
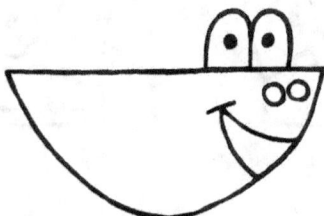
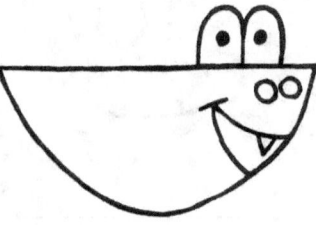

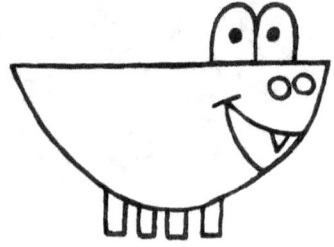
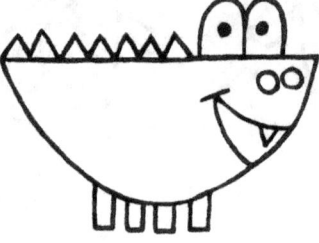

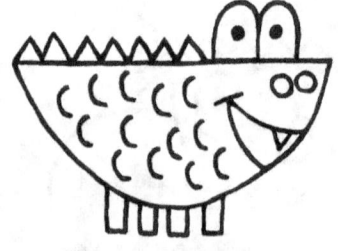

lion

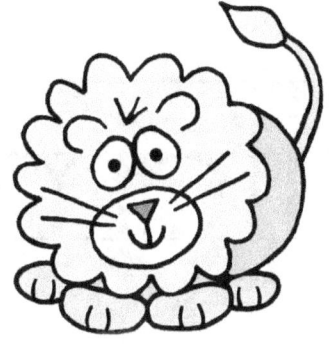

_____

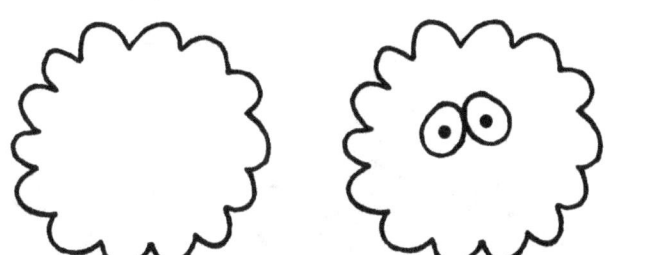 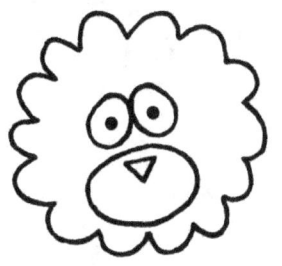 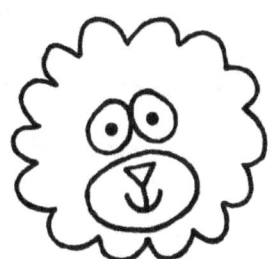

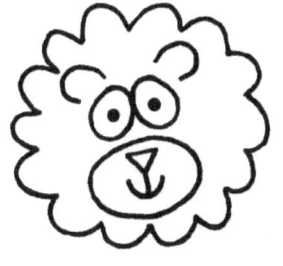 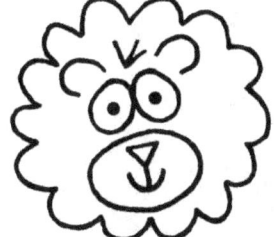 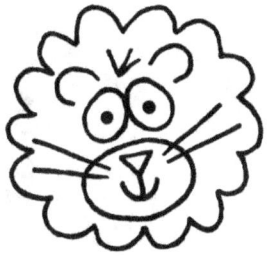

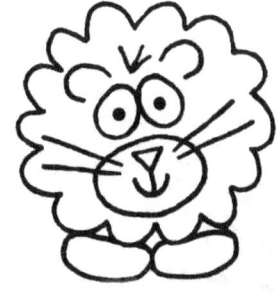 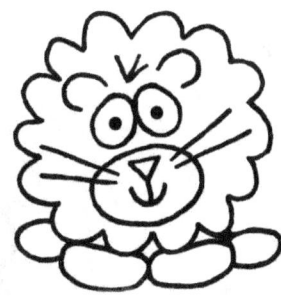 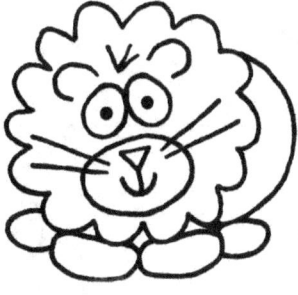

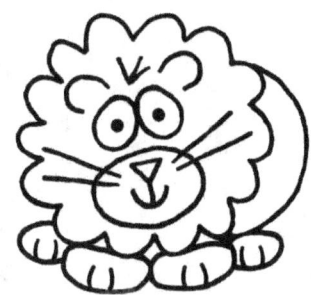 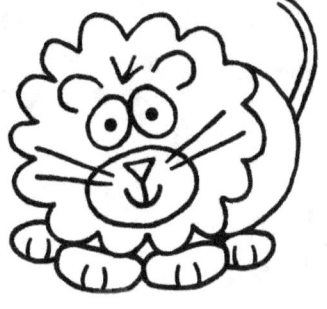 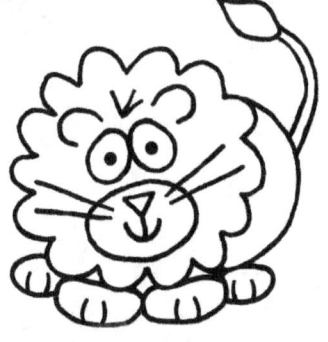

llama

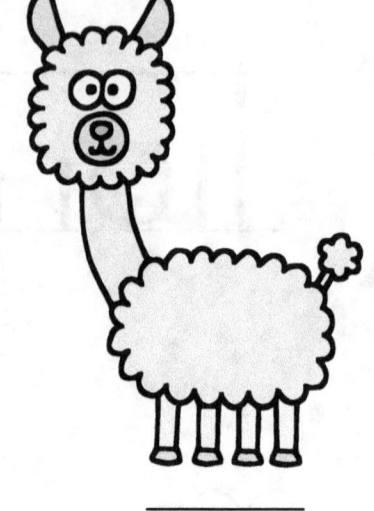

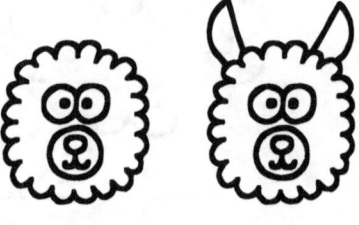

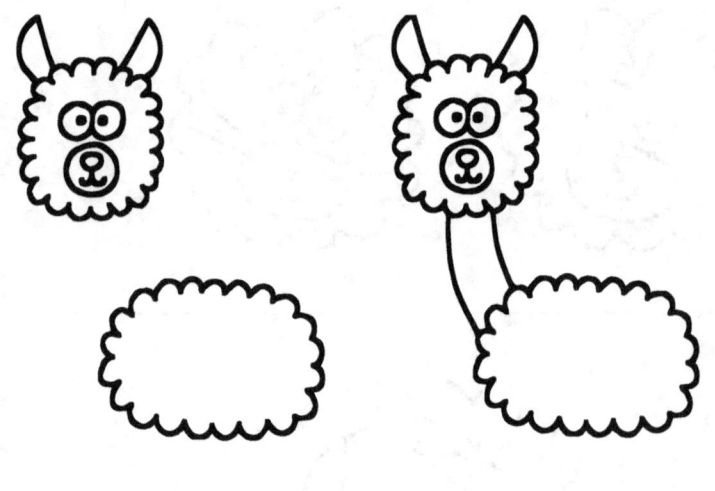

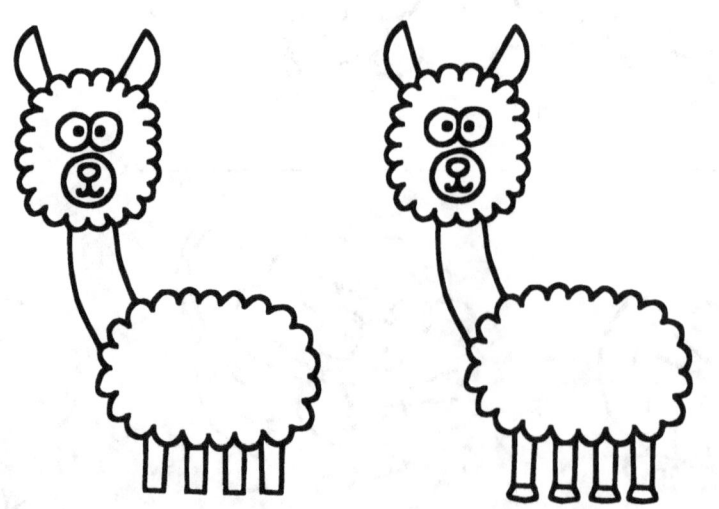
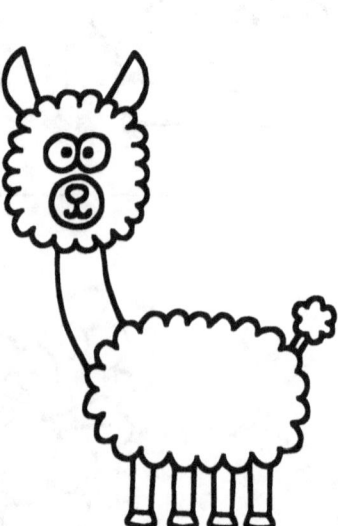

koala

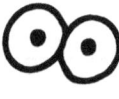 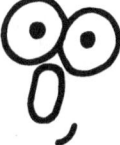 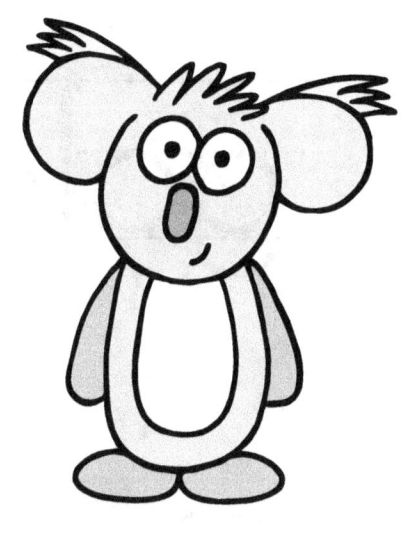

_____

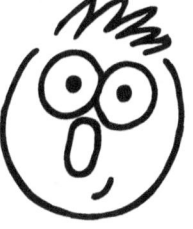 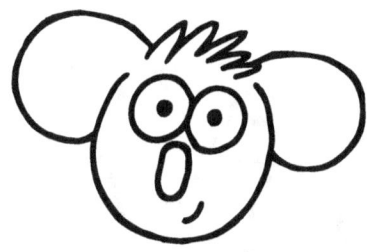 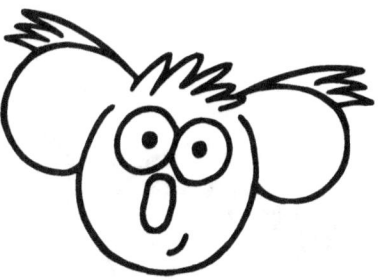

_____   _____

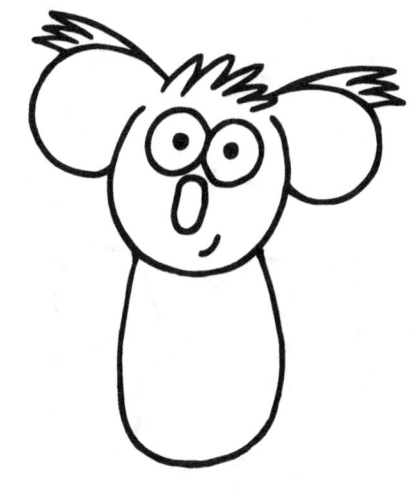 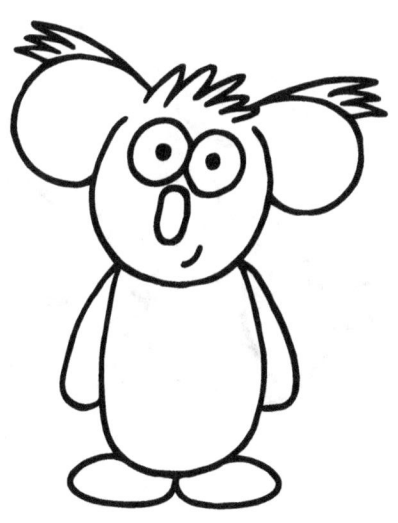 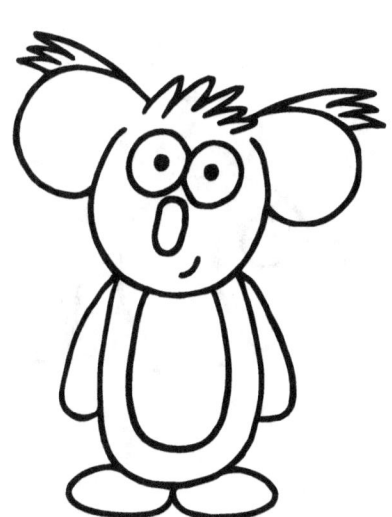

goldfish

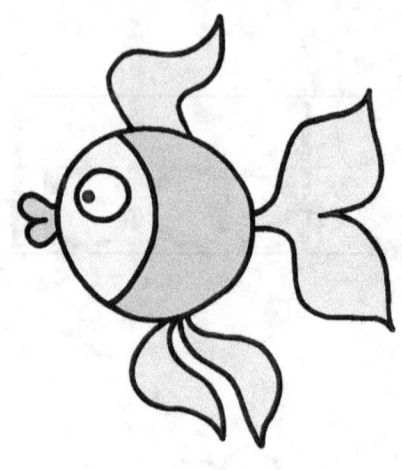

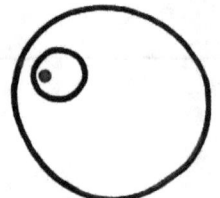
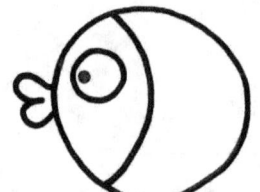

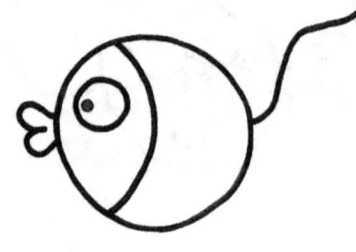
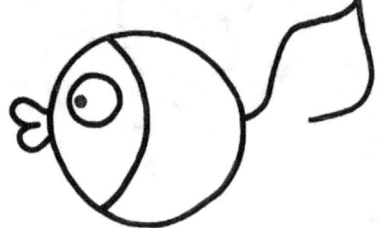
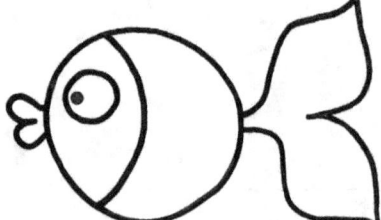

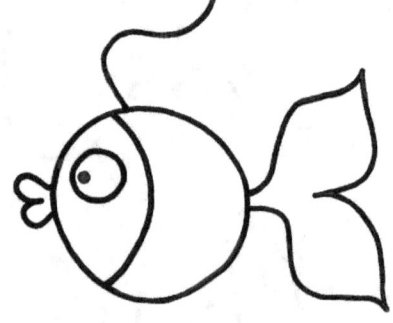
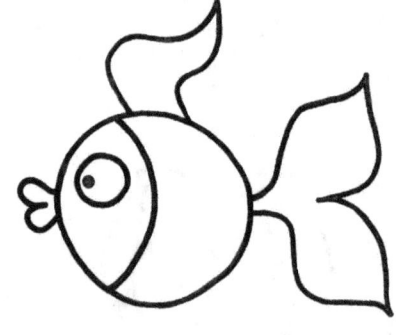
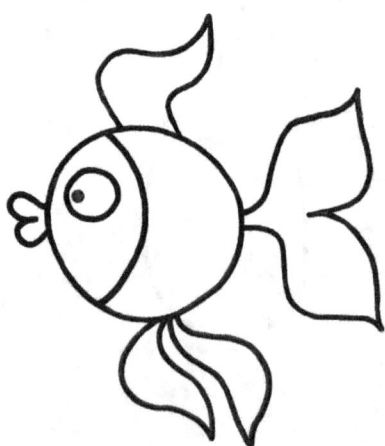

frog

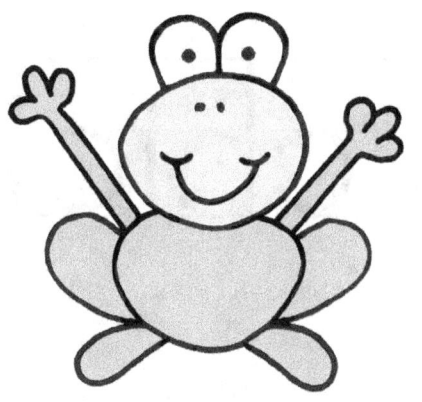

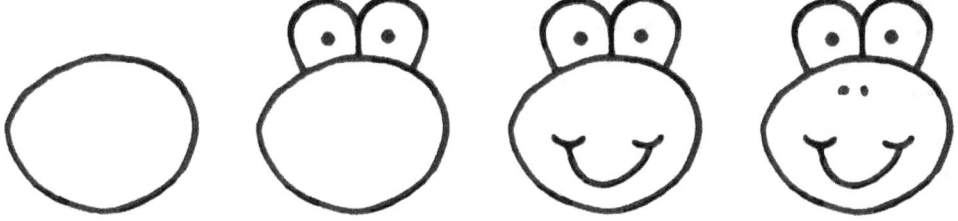

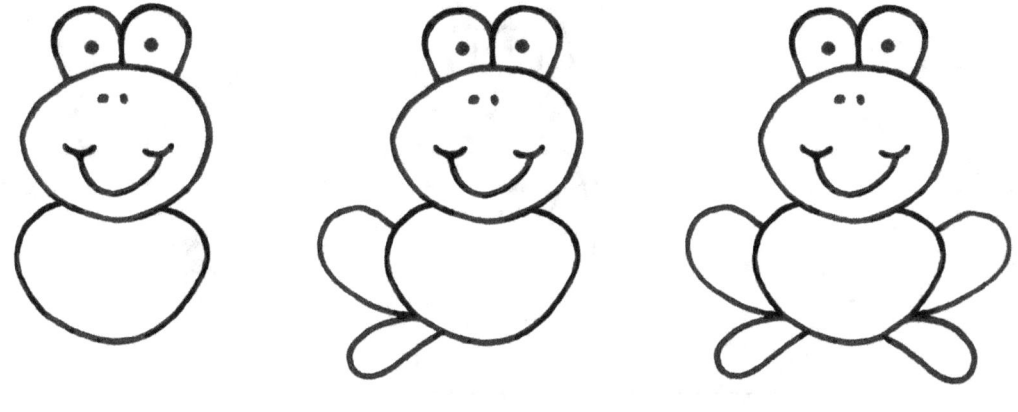

 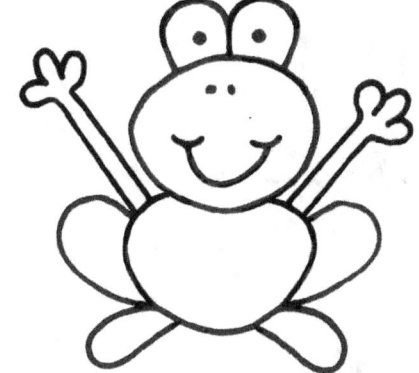

chick

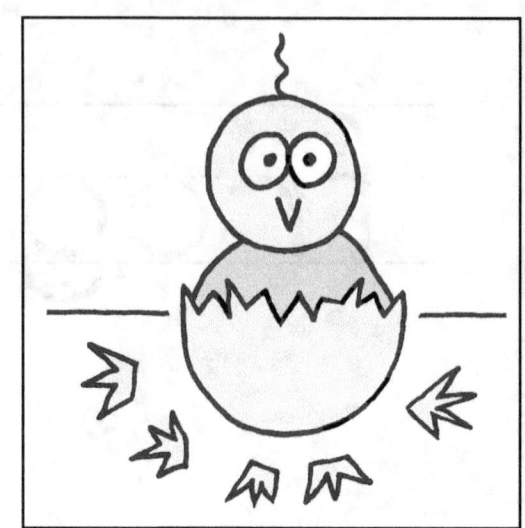

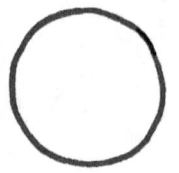 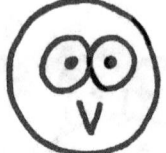 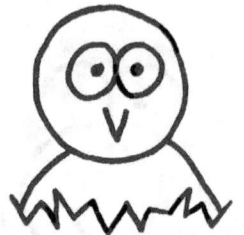

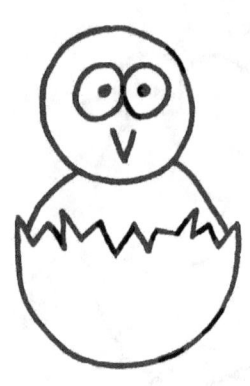 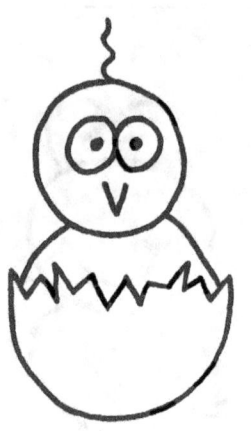 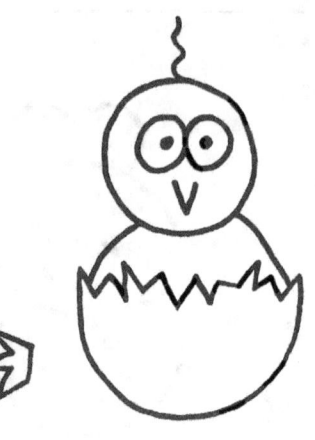

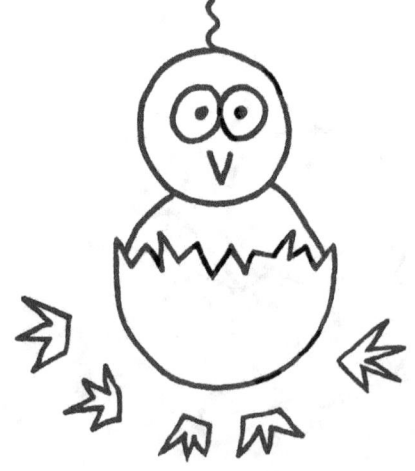 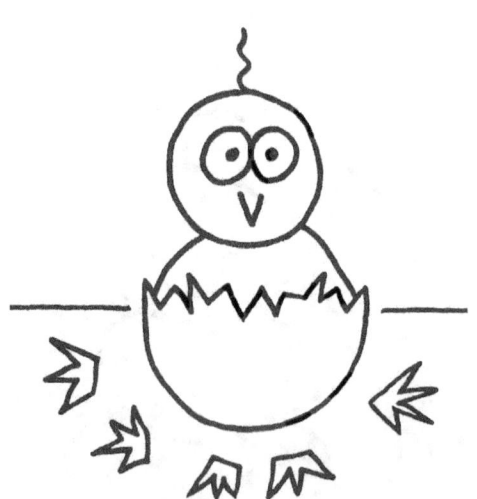

seahorse

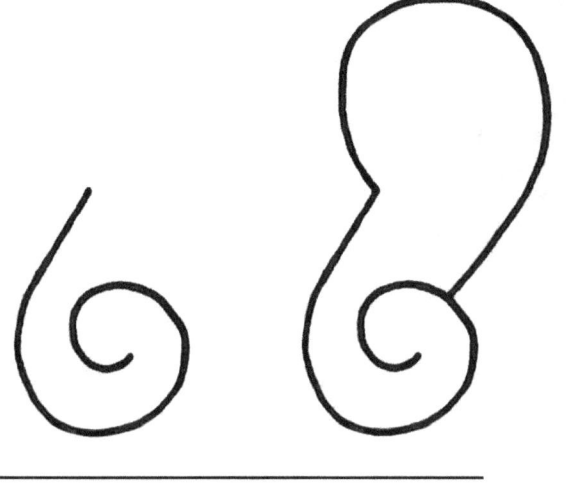

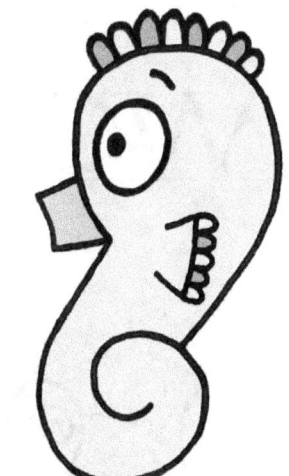

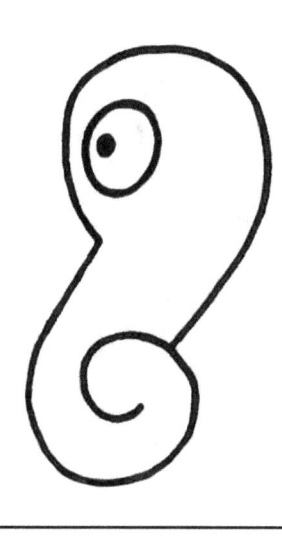
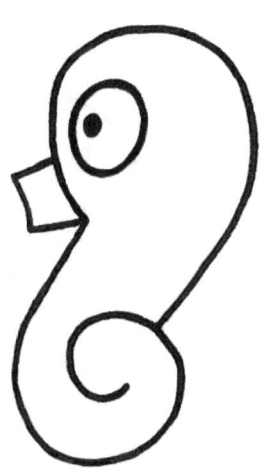

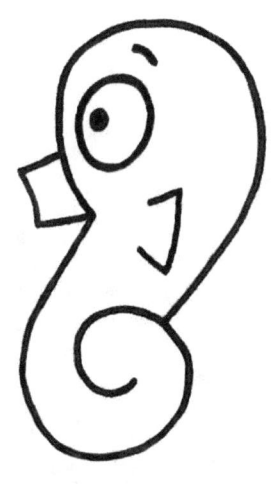
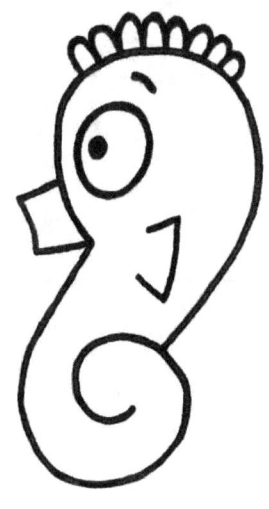
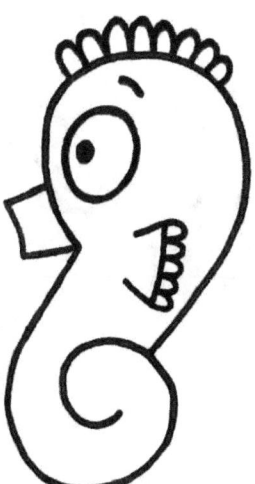

worm

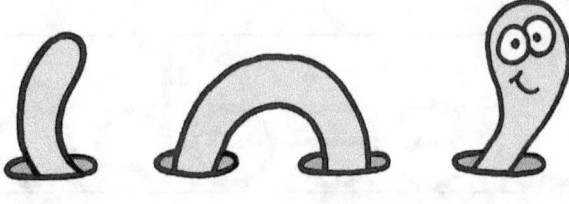

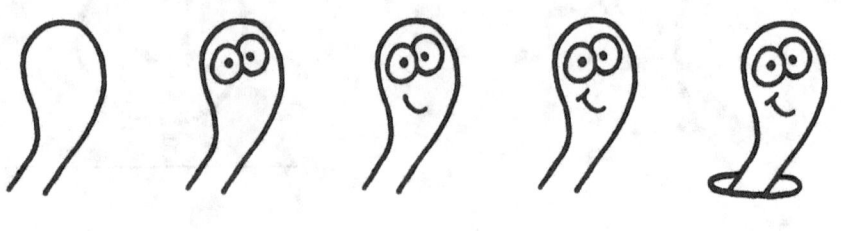

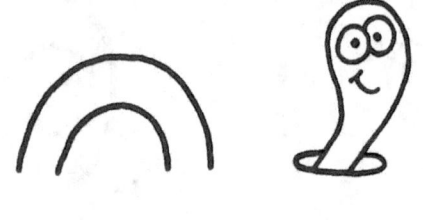

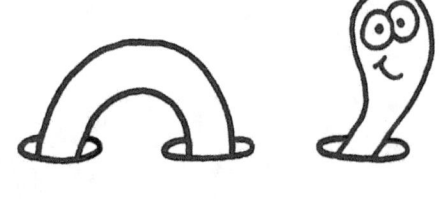

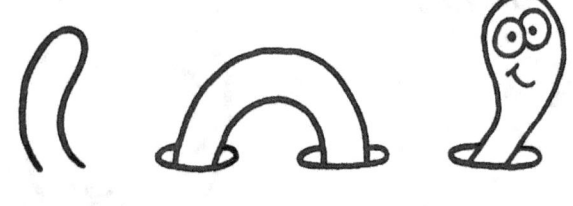

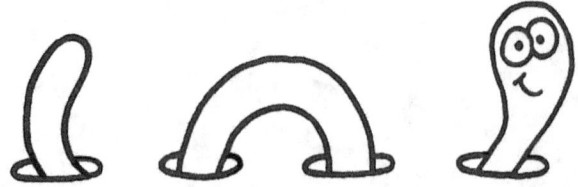

inchworm

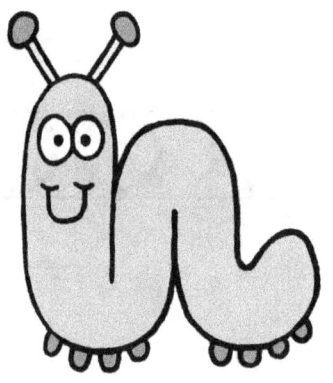

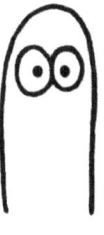 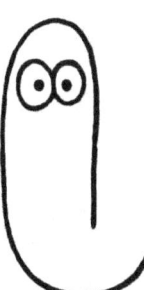 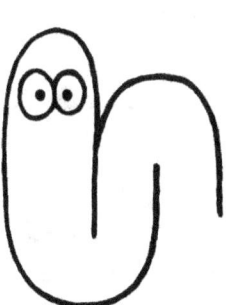 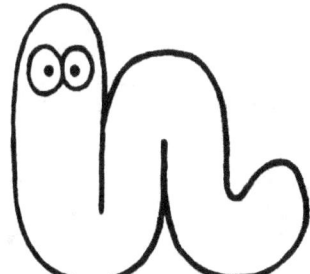

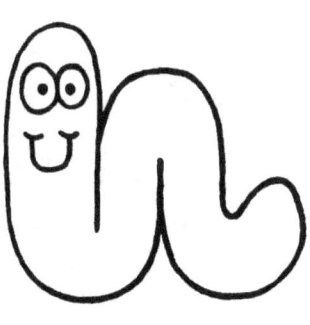 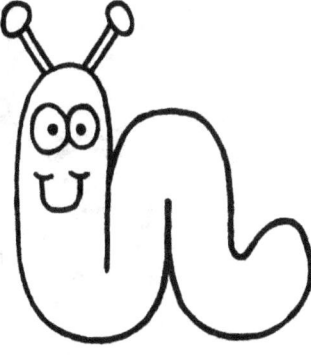

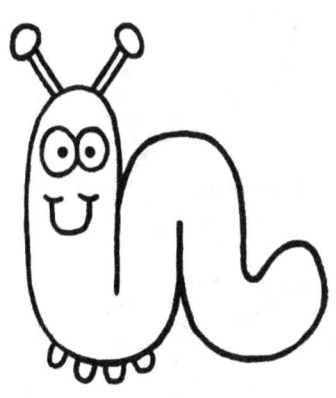 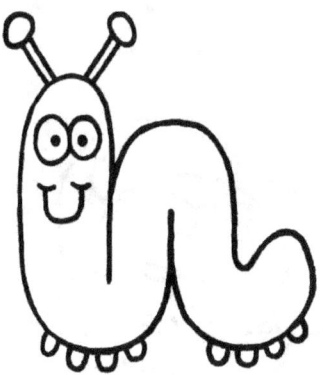

raccoon

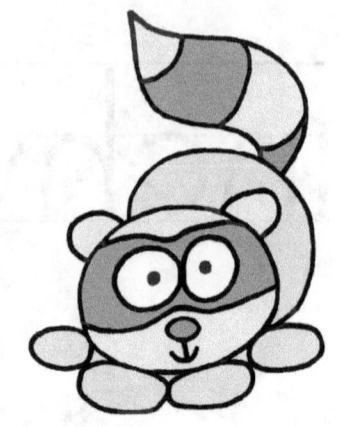

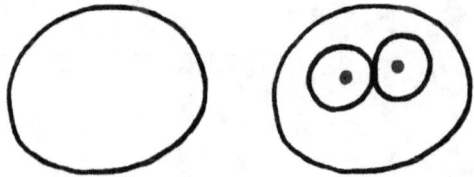

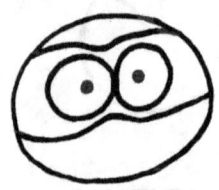 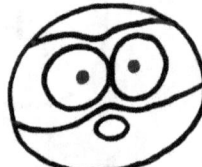 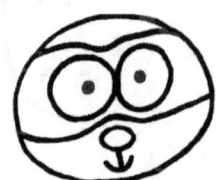 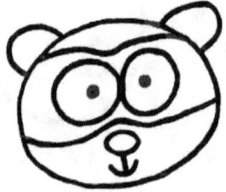

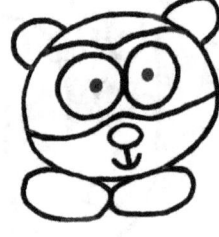 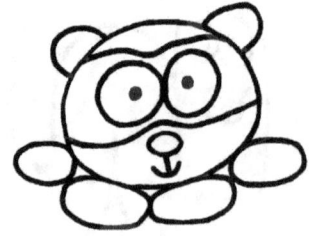

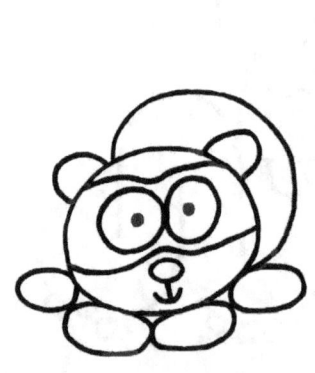 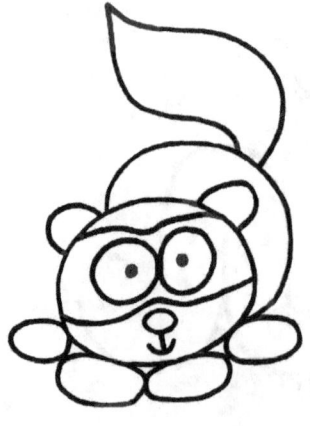 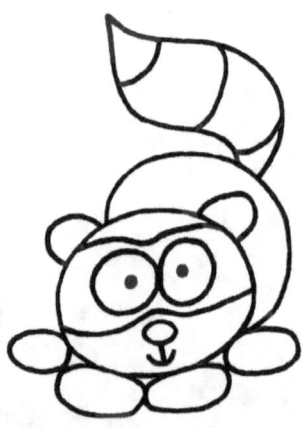

bunny

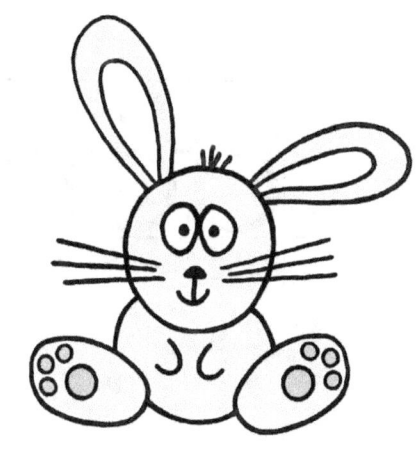

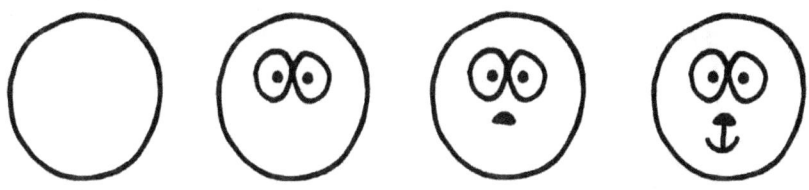

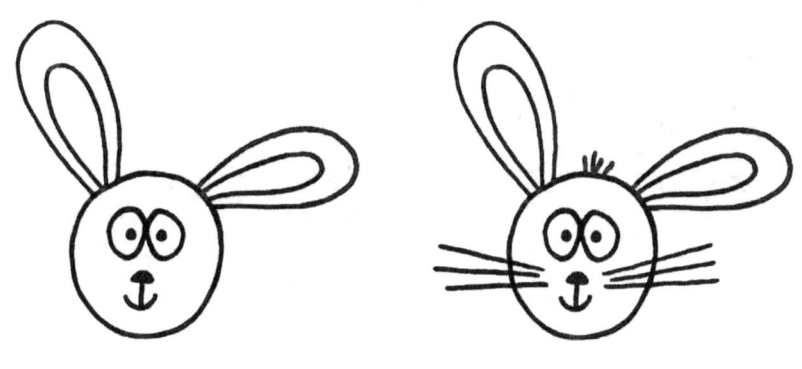

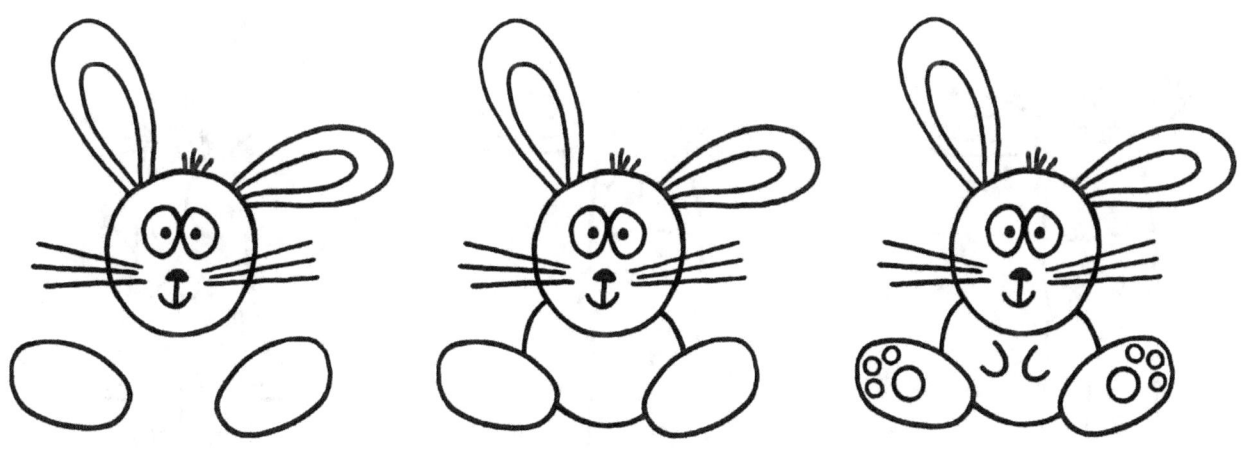

donkey

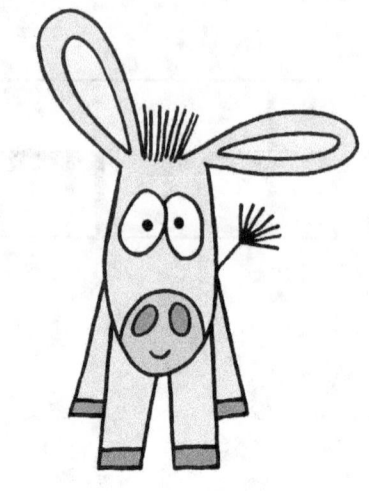

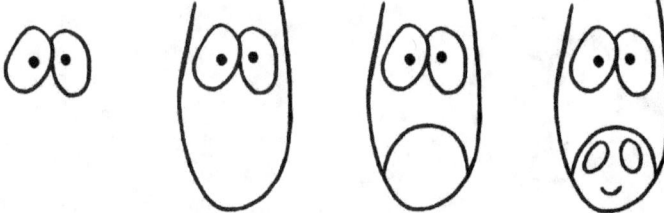

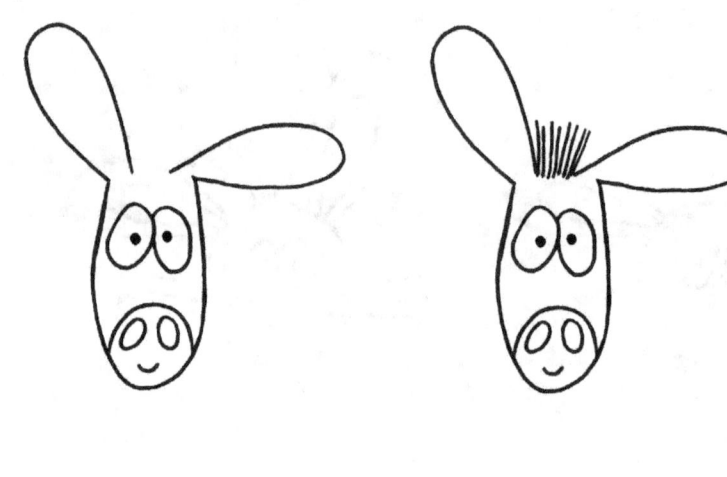

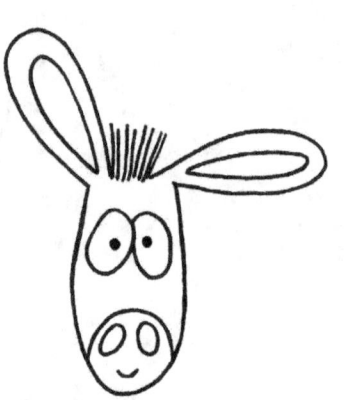

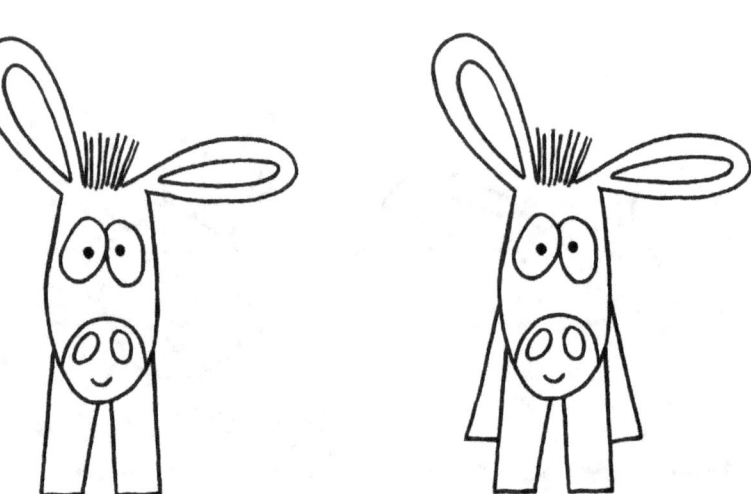

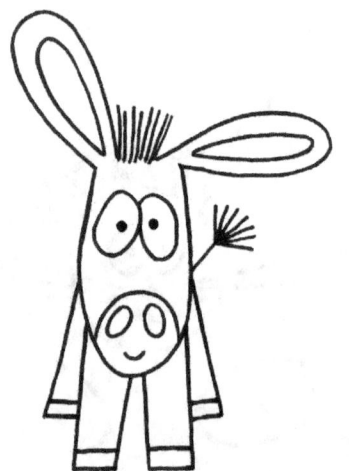

puppy

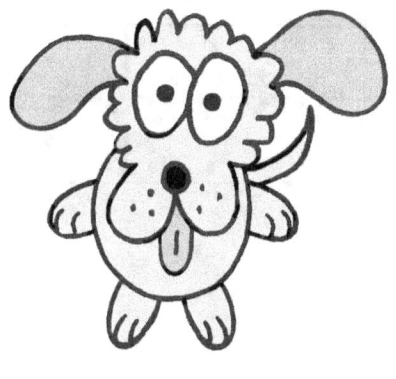

rabbit

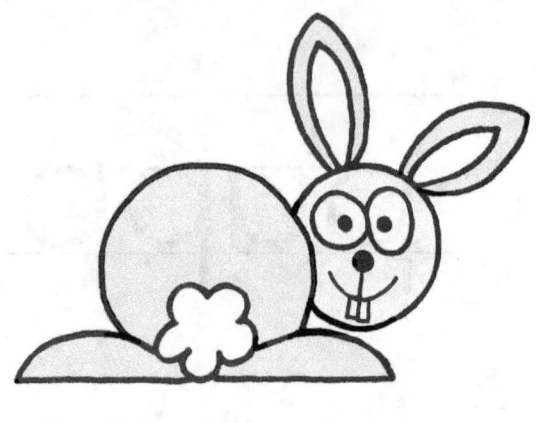

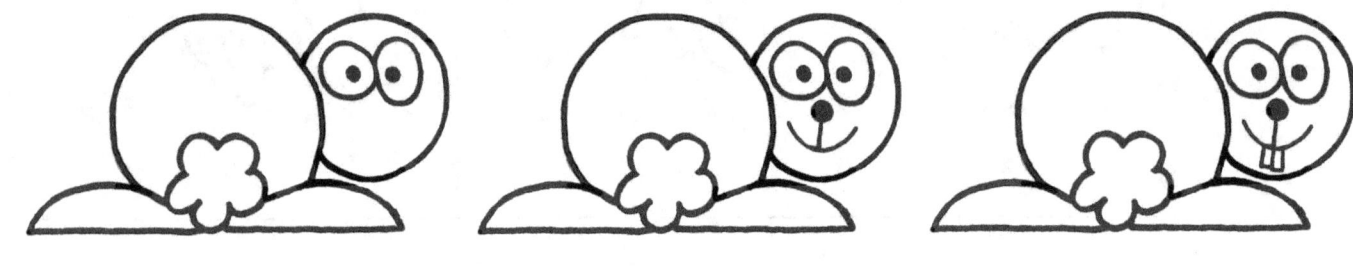

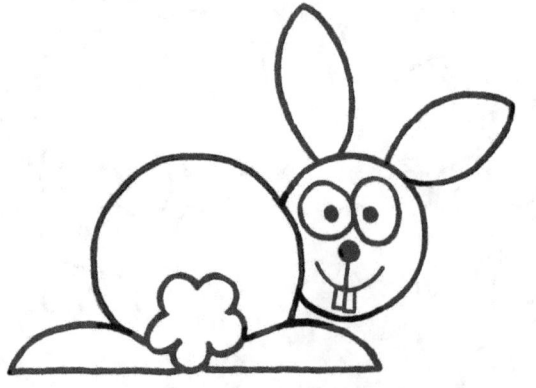

horse

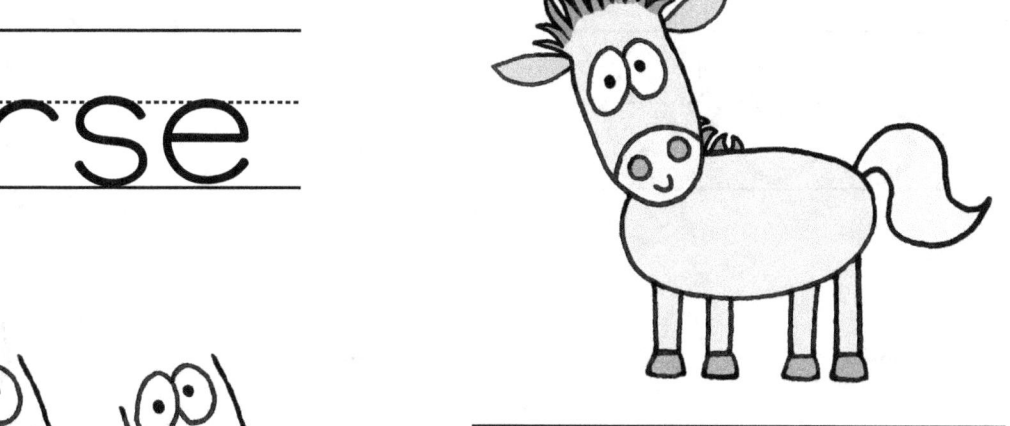

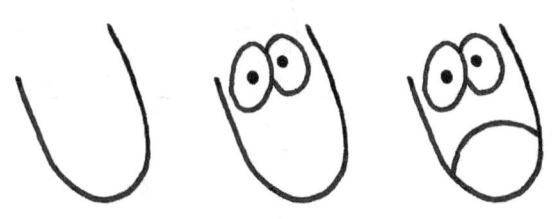

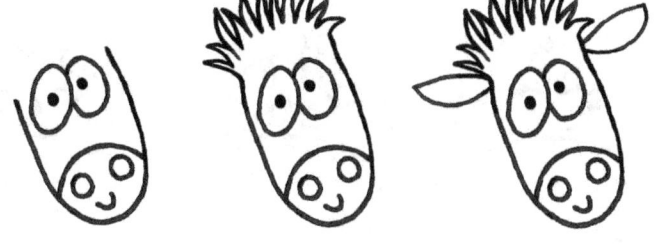

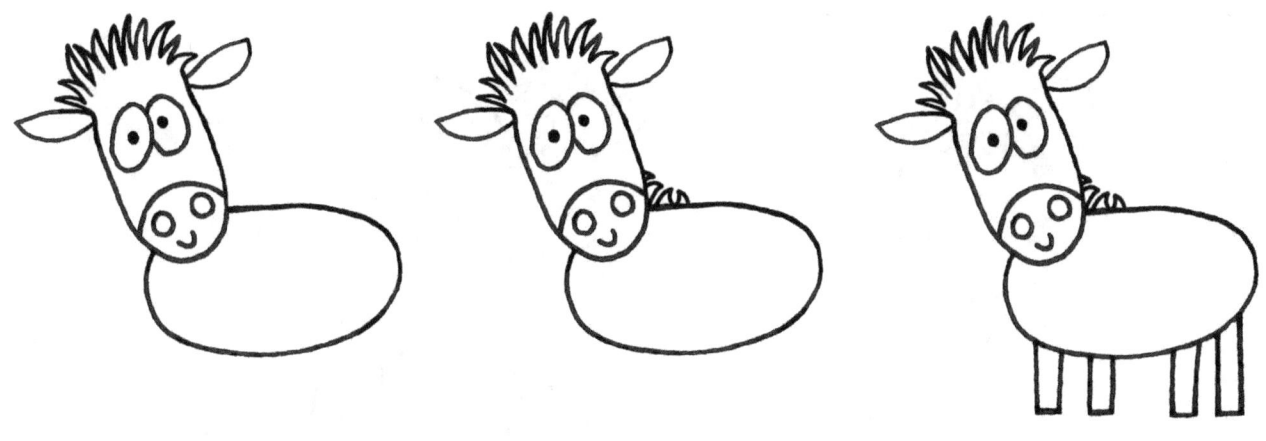

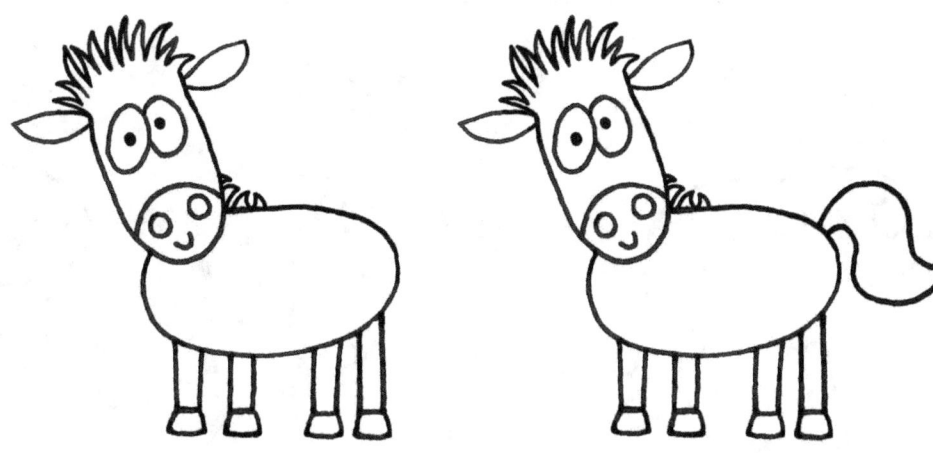

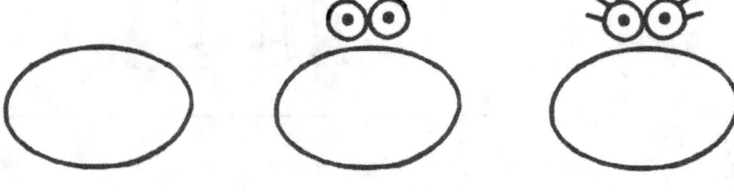

COW

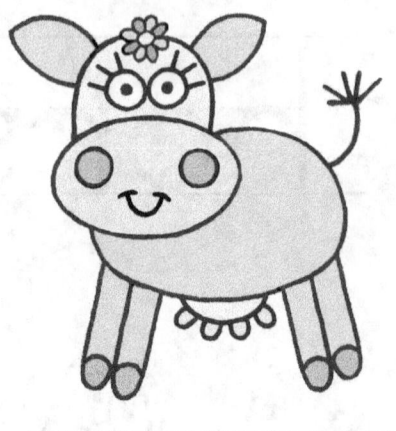

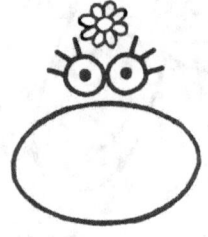 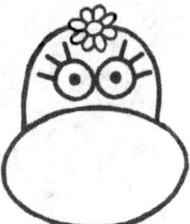 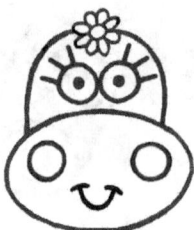 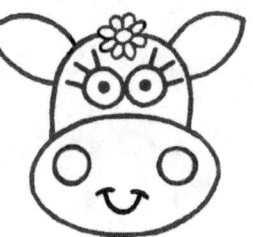

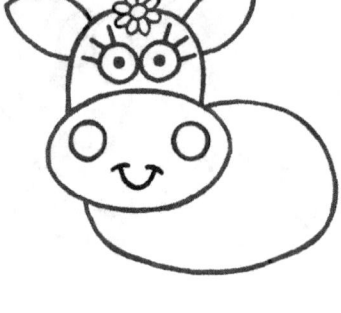 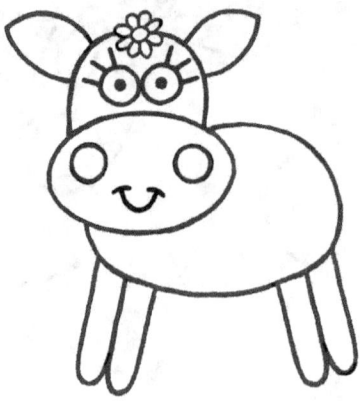

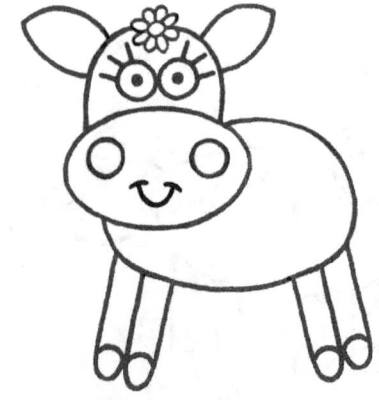 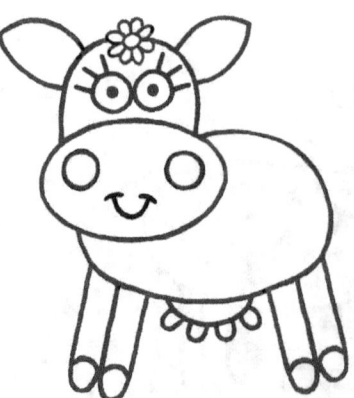 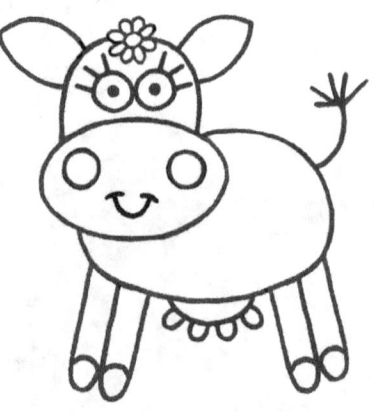

bull

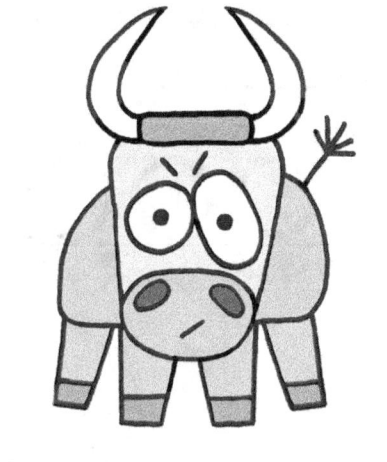

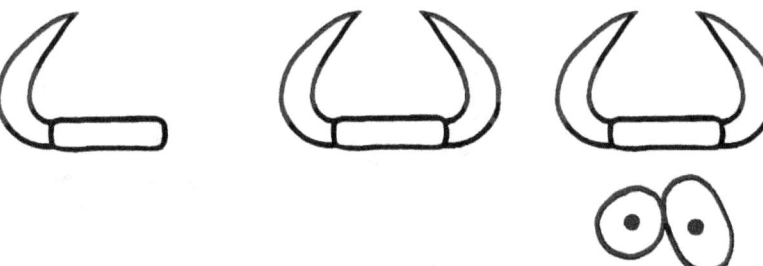

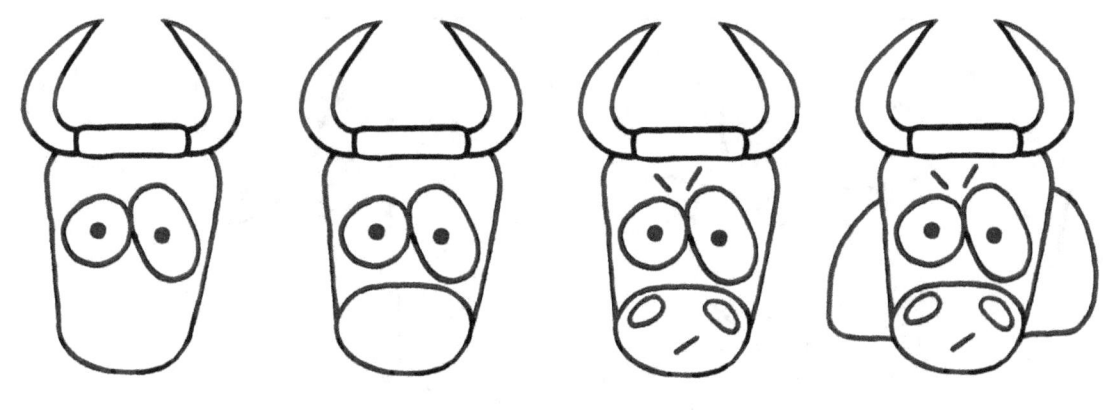

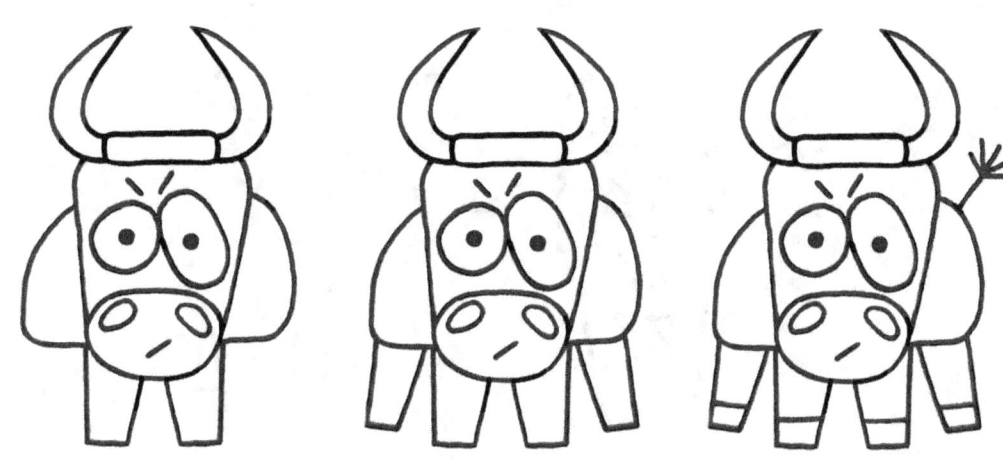

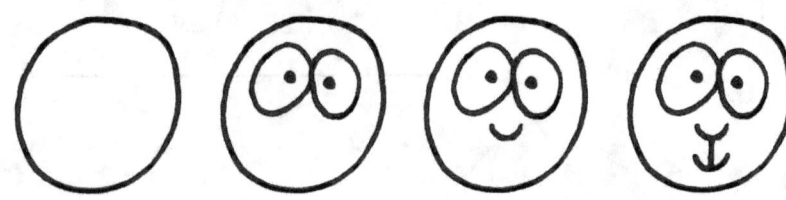

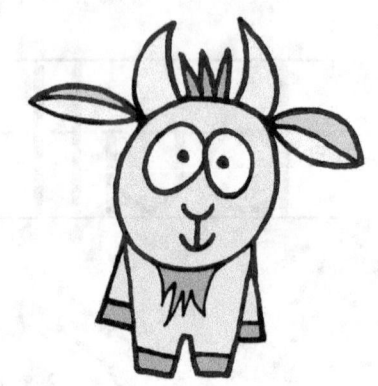

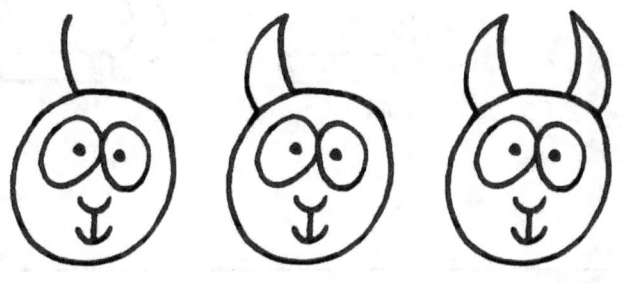

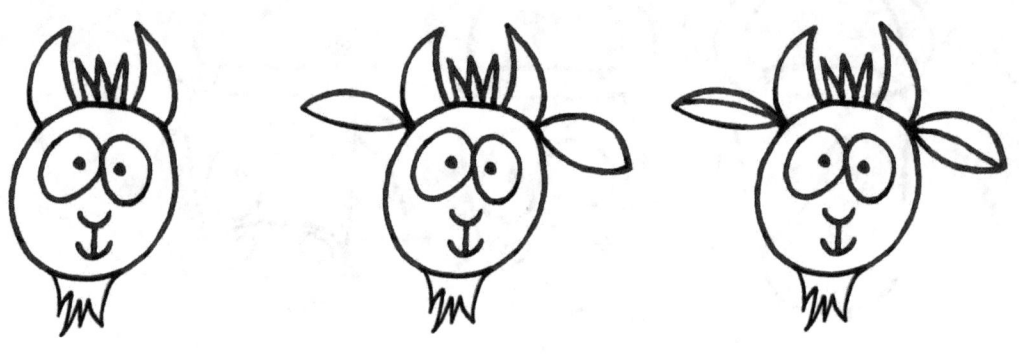

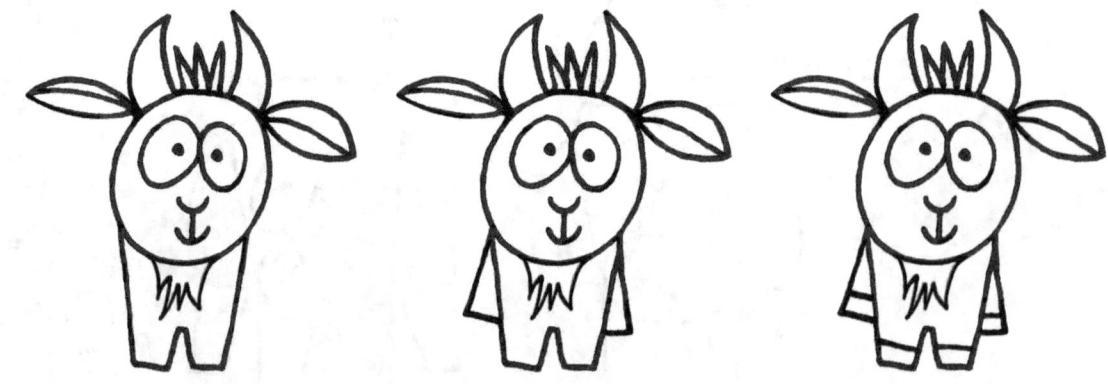

giraffe

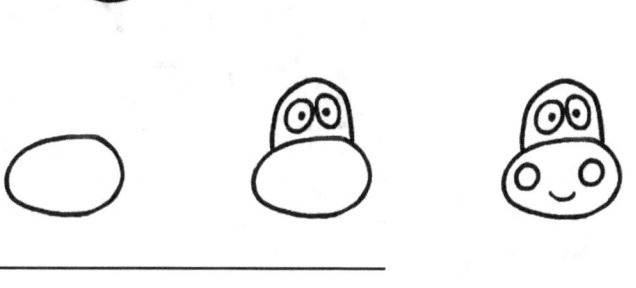

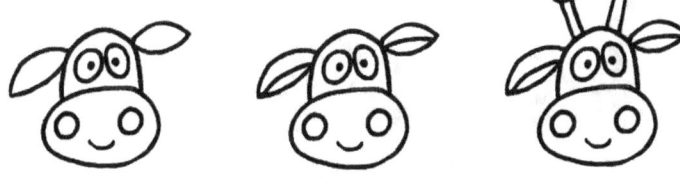

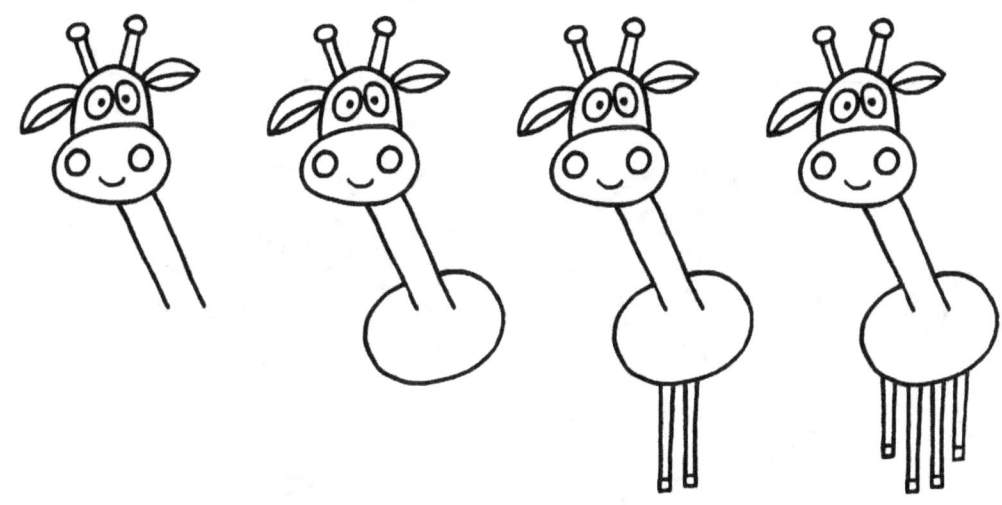

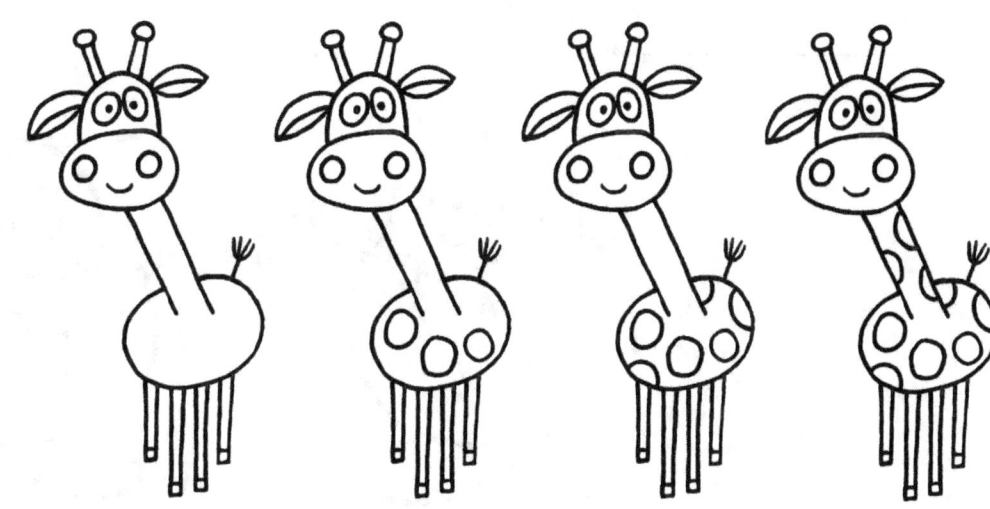

walrus

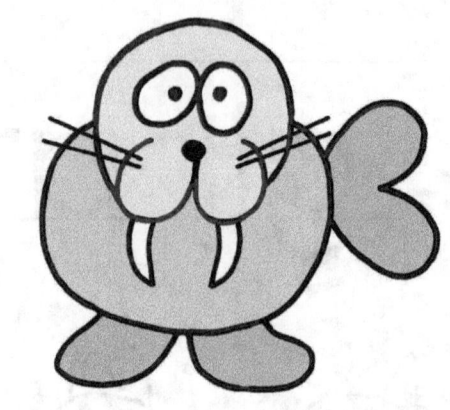

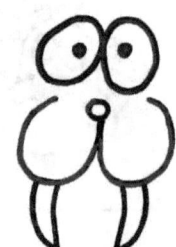 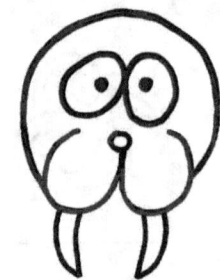

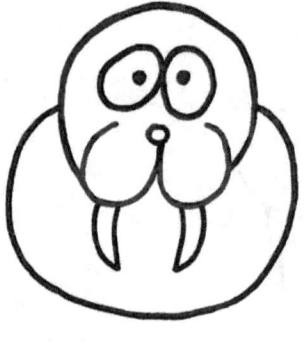 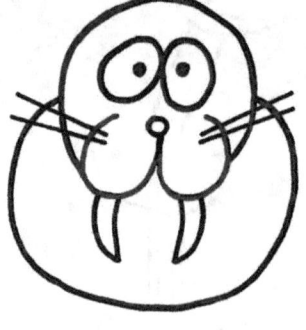 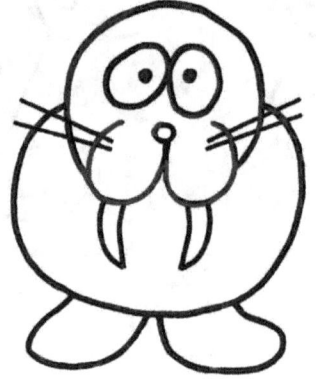

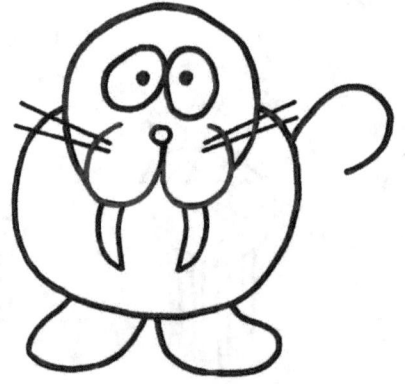 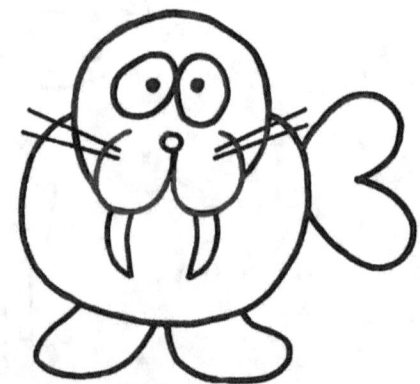

honeybee

_____

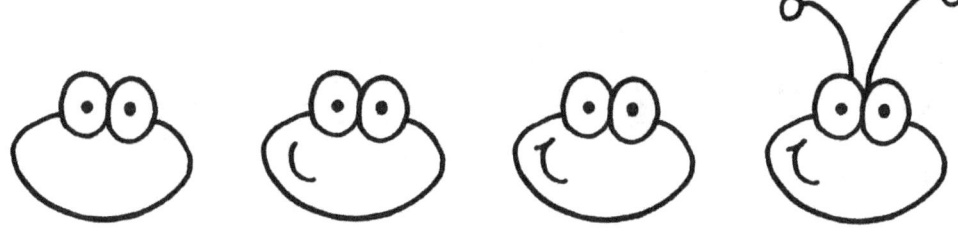

_____

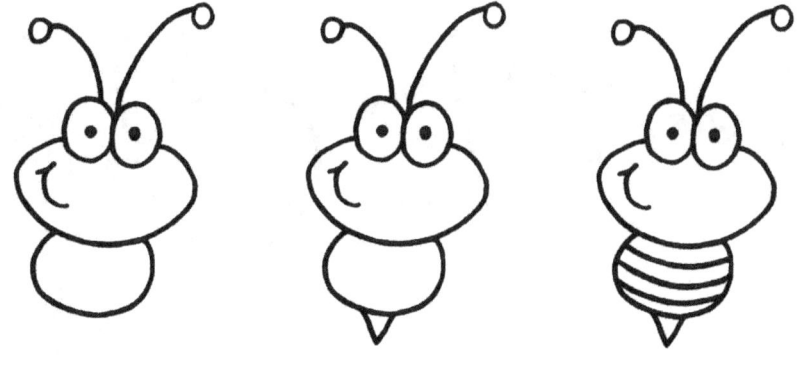

_____

elephant

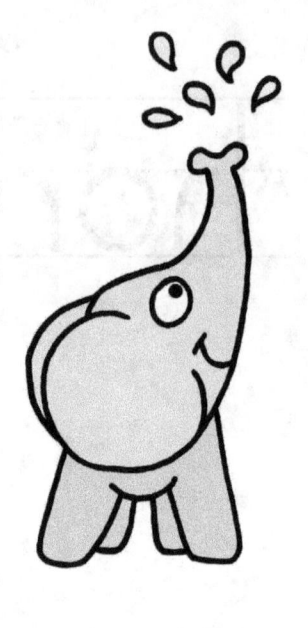

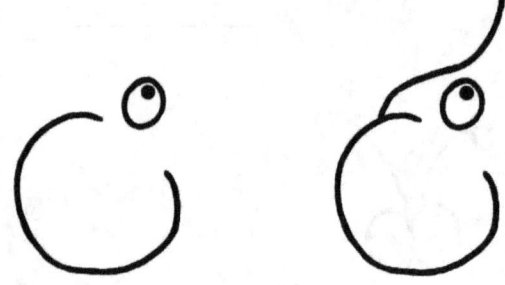

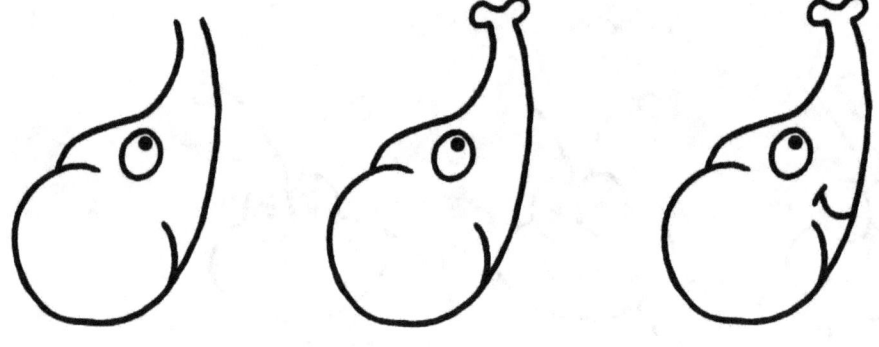

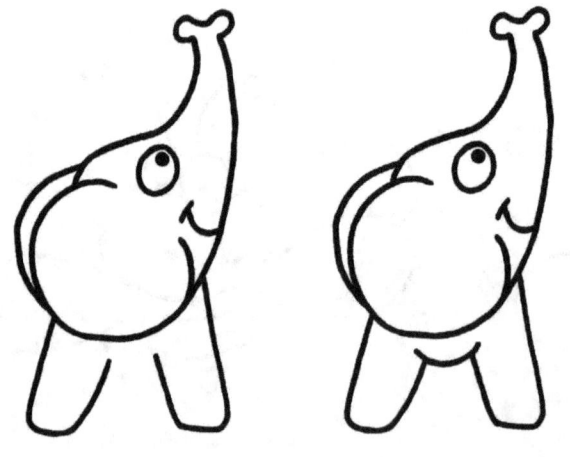 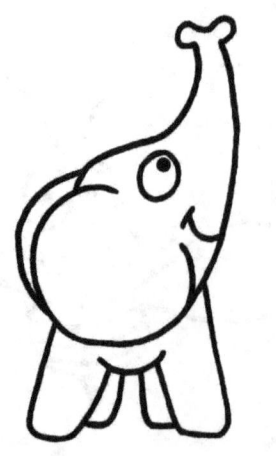 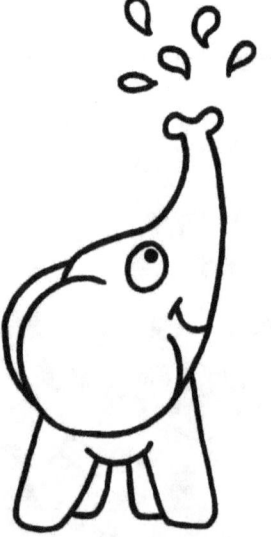

zebra

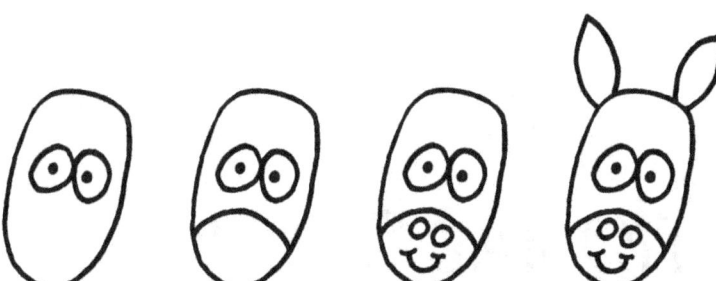
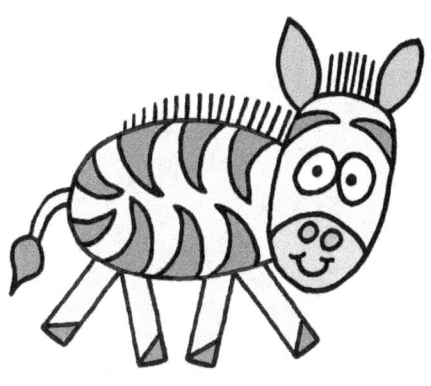

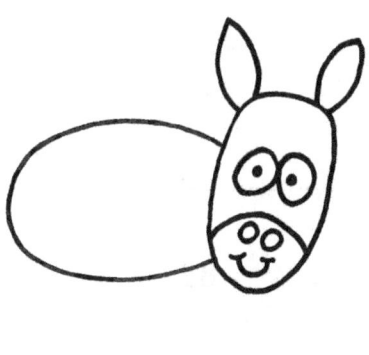
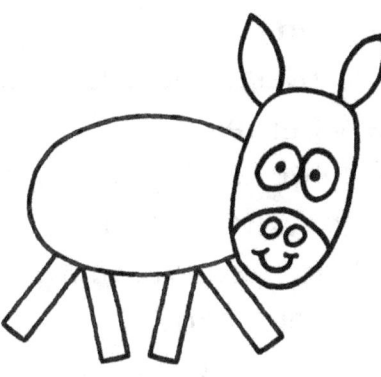
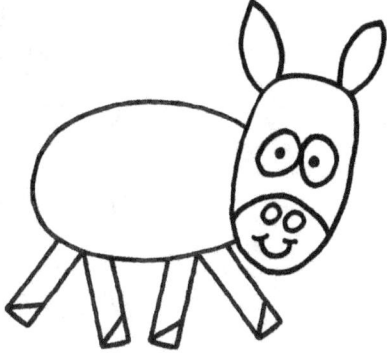

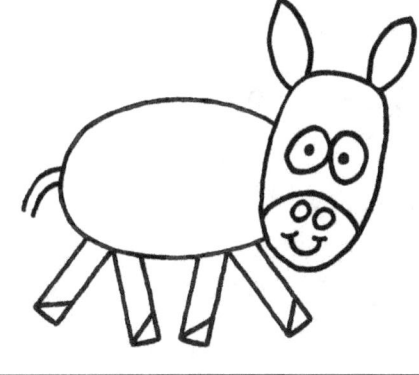
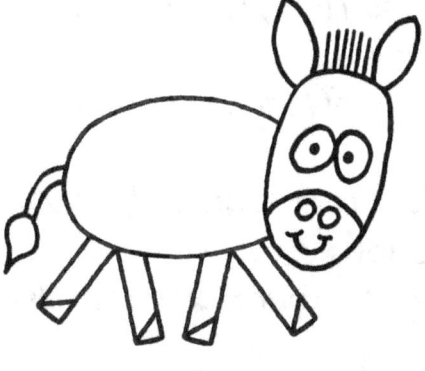
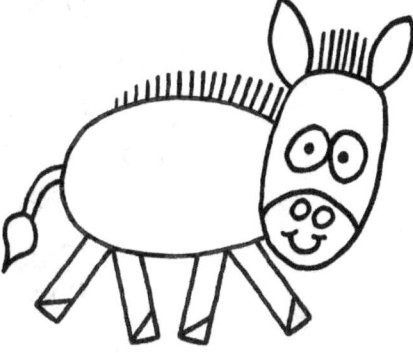

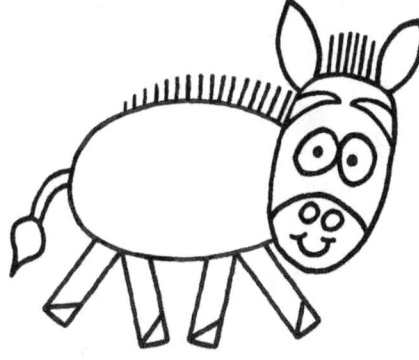
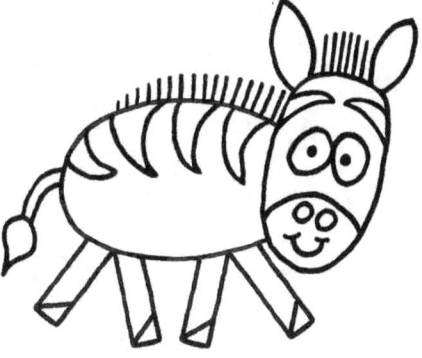
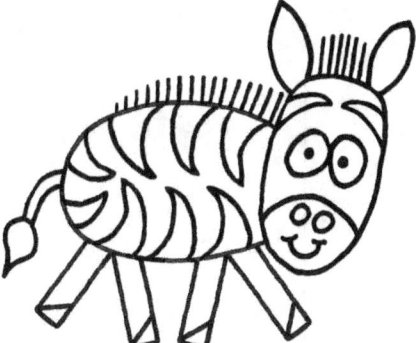

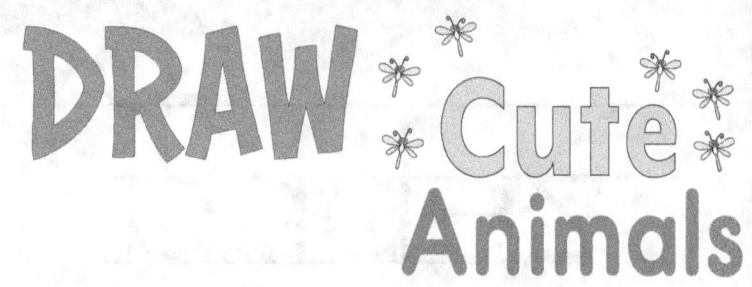

INSTRUCTIONAL GUIDE

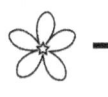

GENERAL LESSON PLAN

WHOLE group & SMALL group

SET EXPECTATIONS for quality student work
Show student work from a previous lesson

DISPLAY the Directed Drawing Lesson for all to see
Optional: keep it out of view as you model

MODEL drawing procedures step by step
Talk through the steps as you draw

PROVIDE students with stationery
Included in this package

CIRCULATE around the class to monitor progress
Give individualized help as needed

CELEBRATE student work
Pause to present some student work in progress

SHOWCASE student work
In a binder, on a bulletin board, assembled into books

SEND HOME to share with families

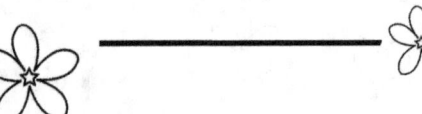 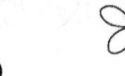 

SET UP
An *easy* and *engaging* Literacy Center

1. DISPLAY
The Directed Drawing Lesson

and a work sample with text

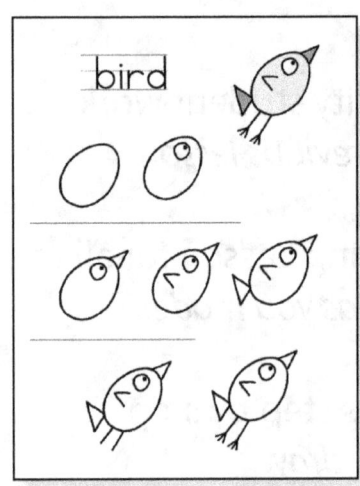

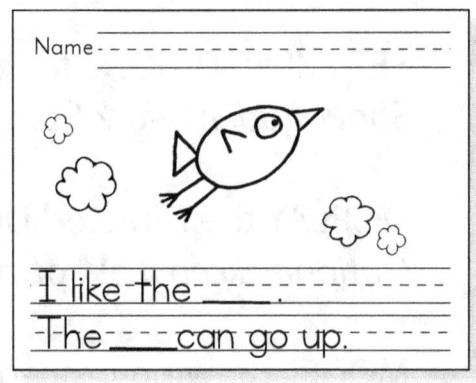

A few Sight Word Sentences can be found on page 7

2. PROVIDE
Stationery with pencils, erasers, and crayons

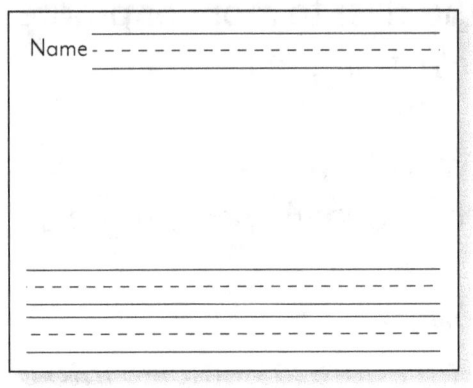

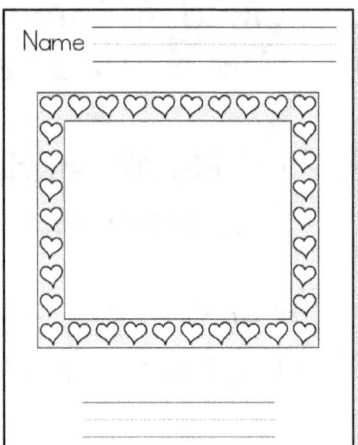

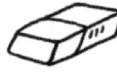 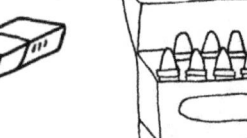

MANY stationery choices are included in this package, pages 72 - 93

3 DONE!

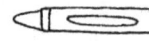

  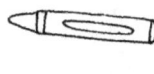

WRITING
with Sight Word Sentences
A Sample for Quick Reference

Level 1

I see the _____. I like the _____.	I like the _____. The _____ can play.	Look at me! I am a _____.
I like the _____. I see the _____ go.	A _____ can play. A _____ can play and play.	Look at my _____. The _____ can go up and up.
I see the _____ go. The _____ can go up.	The _____ and I can play. We like to play and play.	My _____ is big. He is a big _____.
I can see the _____. I like the _____.	I like the _____. We will go play.	I do love the _____. She can play.
We can see the _____. We like the _____.	The _____ and I have to go. We have to go play.	You and I can go see the _____. We will see the _____.
I am a _____. I like to play.	My _____ can play. My _____ and I like to play.	We love the _____. Yes we do.

Level 2

I am good. I am a good _____.	I can run fast. The _____ is fast too.	I want to play. I want to play with my _____.
I am a little _____. Be good to me.	I am here with the _____. I love the _____.	The _____ went out to play.
The _____ is good. She is a good _____.	This is a _____. The _____ can run and	I want to ride a _____. It looks like fun.
Here is a _____. He can play with me all	This is my _____. She is a good friend to me.	The _____ is going away. That is okay.
We will play with the _____.	The _____ has a little friend. That friend is me.	You are pretty. You are a pretty little
They can see the _____. They like the _____.	Come with me, little _____. You are my friend.	The _____ is happy. Today is a good day.

Questions

I see the _____ play. Can you see the _____ play?	I am a good little _____. Will you be my friend?	Who likes the _____? We all like the _____.
I love my _____. Do you love my _____?	I will go see the _____. Will you go too?	What did the _____ do? It played and played all day.

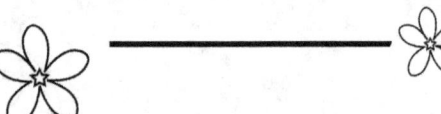

SCRIPT

An example of what I typically say while
giving a Directed Drawing Lesson.

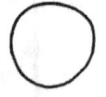
*Everybody draw a **circle** in the **middle** of your paper. Start
here and draw it all the way **around**. Now the circle is
closed. It is a **closed shape**.*

*Now I want you to draw two **circles** for eyes, just like this.*

*Put one **dot** right in the **middle** of each eye.*

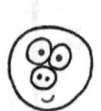
*Now we are going to draw the pig's nose. **Below** the eyes
draw a **circle**, like this. Put two dots **inside** the circle to
finish the pig's nose.*

*Draw a **curve** under the nose to make the pig smile.*

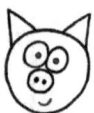
*And now for the ears. Draw an **angle** to make each ear,
like this. These are not a **triangles** because **triangles** have
three **straight lines** and these shapes have two **straight
lines** and a **curve**.*

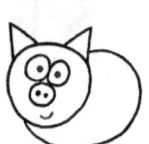
*So let's put a couple of **angles on top of** the head, like this.
{Optional} Put a **point** where you think the **tip** of the ear
should go. Now draw two **lines** down all the way to **the
top of** the head.*

*Draw a big **curve** for the body **on the right**.*

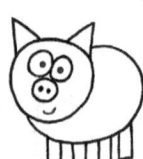
*Now for the legs. They look like **rectangles** but are not.
Rectangles have four straight lines. The **top** of each leg is
not a **straight line** because it is the **curve** of the body.*

*Draw two **straight lines** down. Now **close the shape** with
a **straight line** for a **base**.*

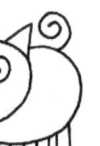
Draw four legs.

*Put a **spiral** for a tail just where it belongs, like this.*

Now let's color!

LOTS of vocabulary, right?

Pause after this first step
to make sure the kids get
the shape right and placed
appropriately on the page.
Some kids will not close
the shape, others will
make it very small, some
will put it too close to the
edge of the paper and will
not be able to squeeze the
animal's body onto the
page etc....

Draw a triangle to show what
one looks like. Point out the
three straight lines. Point out
the angles. Count the sides
and count the angles.

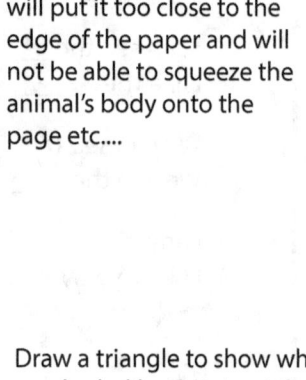

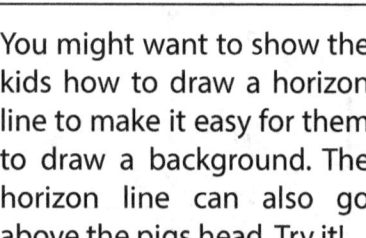

You might want to show the
kids how to draw a horizon
line to make it easy for them
to draw a background. The
horizon line can also go
above the pigs head. Try it!

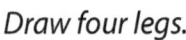

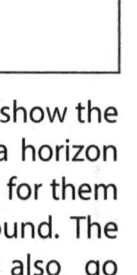

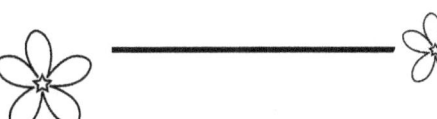 

LINES
and SHAPES
Fundamental Early Geometry

Take a look at our friendly pig.

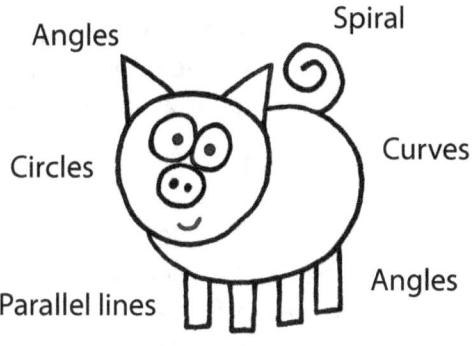

Angles   Spiral

Circles   Curves

Parallel lines   Angles

Perpendicular lines

LINES

straight
curved
scalloped
zigzag
spiral

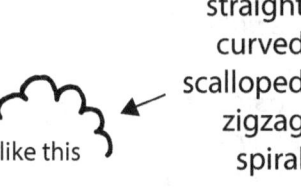

like this

diagonal
horizontal
vertical

parallel
perpendicular

Line Descriptors

wavy   dotted
jagged   dashed
bouncy   thick
wiggly   thin
crooked
curly
loopy
graceful
scribbly
tapered
crosshatched

SHAPES

Circle
Oval
Semi-circle
Angle
Triangle
Teardrop
Crescent
Rectangle
Square
Trapezoid
Rhombus

Shape Descriptors

closed
open
vertex
side

amorphous
blob

Rectilinear Shapes

Triangles appear in this series, as tails on birds and fish mostly. Squares, rectangles, rhombuses, and trapezoids appear in only a few places in the Draw Cute Animals series. For example, as hooves. However, these shapes can be incorporated quite easily into your student's drawings as features of landscape. Add a sign, for example.

Or a simple shed.

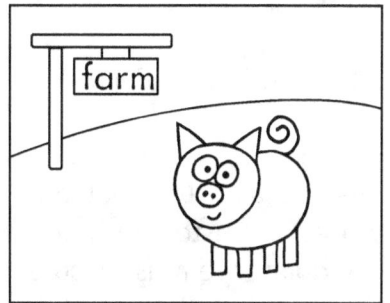

The horizon line can also go above the pigs head. Try it.

You can easily find landscape examples by using appropriate terms. Search *gate cartoon* or *fence illustration.* Use words such as *cute, kids, kindergarten, icon,* and *simple* to narrow your search. You will quickly find images to inspire you. Teach your kids to do the same.

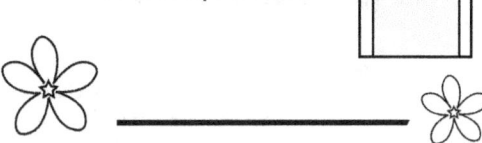 

POSITION WORDS

PREPOSITIONS OF PLACE, TIME, AND MOVEMENT

Position words are prepositions that are used to indicate place, time, and movement. Use these terms as you give your lessons, and encourage your students to use them to describe their drawings. Over time your students will come to know exactly what they mean.

Above	*Before*	*In*	*On*	*Throughout*
Across	*Behind*	*In back of*	*On the bottom of*	*To the right of*
Across from	*Below*	*In between*	*On top of*	*To the left of*
After	*Beneath*	*In front of*	*Onto*	*To the side of*
Against	*Beside*	*In the center of*	*Opposite to*	*Together with*
Ahead of	*Between*	*In the middle of*	*Out*	*Toward/towards*
Along	*Beyond*	*Inside*	*Out of*	*Under*
Along with	*By*	*Inside of*	*Outside*	*Underneath*
Alongside	*Close to*	*Into*	*Outside of*	*Up against*
Among	*Far*	*Near*	*Over*	*Up to*
Apart from	*Far from*	*Near to*	*Past*	*Upon*
Around	*Here*	*Next to*	*There*	*With*
Away from		*Off*	*Through*	*Within*

Math Vocabulary and Informal Colloquial Language

There is a difference between the precisely defined, strict vocabulary used in mathematics, and the informal vocabulary used in everyday colloquial speech.

Spiral is a mathematical term, but *curl* is not. *Point* is a mathematical term, but *dot* is not.

As teachers of mathematics we must ensure that our students know the vocabulary used in customary math instruction. And as teachers of language we must ensure that our students learn the informal vocabulary used in everyday speech.

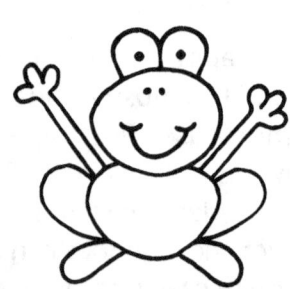

It may be worth consulting your school's adopted math program for the mathematical language used in your district.

TIPS

DRAWING Tips

HELP students to draw larger pictures by drawing the first step for them - some children tend to draw their pictures very small.

CONSIDER limiting students to pencils and erasers during the whole group lesson. Coloring can come afterwards.

SHOW students how to draw a horizon line.

TEACH students about pencil pressure; press the pencil lightly or heavily for different effects.

DEMONSTRATE eye pupil placement to indicate a look to the left, right, up, or down.

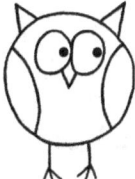 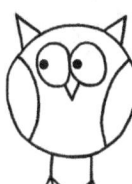

Literacy Center Ideas

TEACH a few Directed Drawing Lessons to the whole group before students try new lessons independently at the Literacy Center.

USE math language such as rectangle, direction, curve, angle, semi-circle, above, below etc... as you model drawing.

MAKE an EASEL by standing up a three ring binder and clipping the Directed Drawing Lesson to it.

CONNECT the Cute Animal with a story, a theme, a process, or any other curricular content you are currently teaching.

POSE a question to prompt a written response.

PROVIDE a Sight Word Sentence for students to copy.

MAINTAIN a three ring binder of exemplary student work at the Literacy Center for other students to read, copy, and be inspired by.

COMPILE your own drawings from your Directed Drawing Lessons into a book or folder to place at the Literacy Center for students to peruse.

POST your own drawings at the Literacy Center for students to copy.

KEEP a folder of previous lessons at the Literacy Center for students to try again.

Stationery

10 Writing Templates

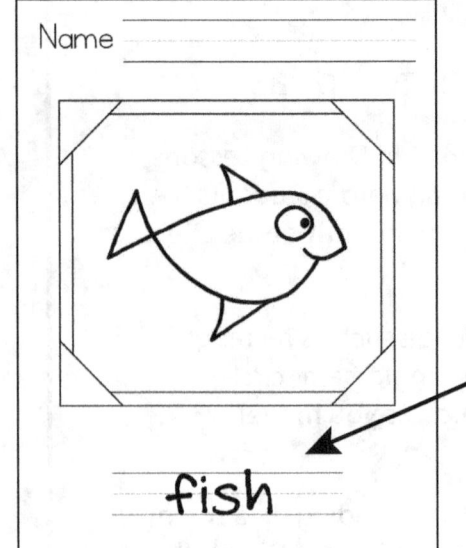

Name

fish

Write the Cute Animal name

Art Sheets

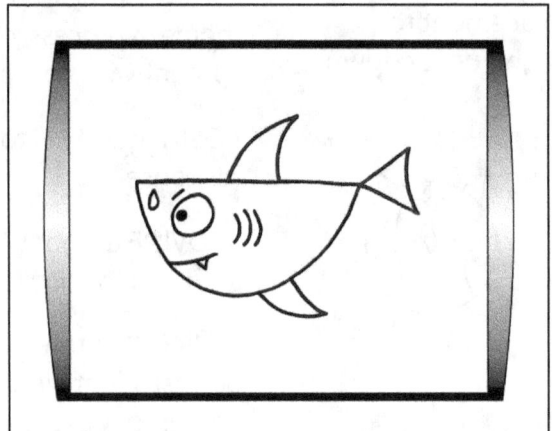

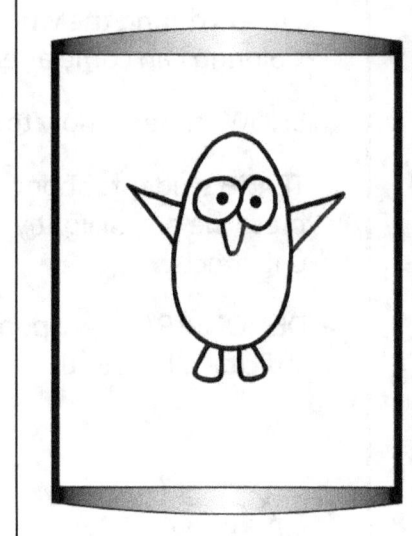

Two Orientations

Kindergarten LANDSCAPE
    3-4 words per line

Name

Name

Name

one line

two lines

three lines

Name _____

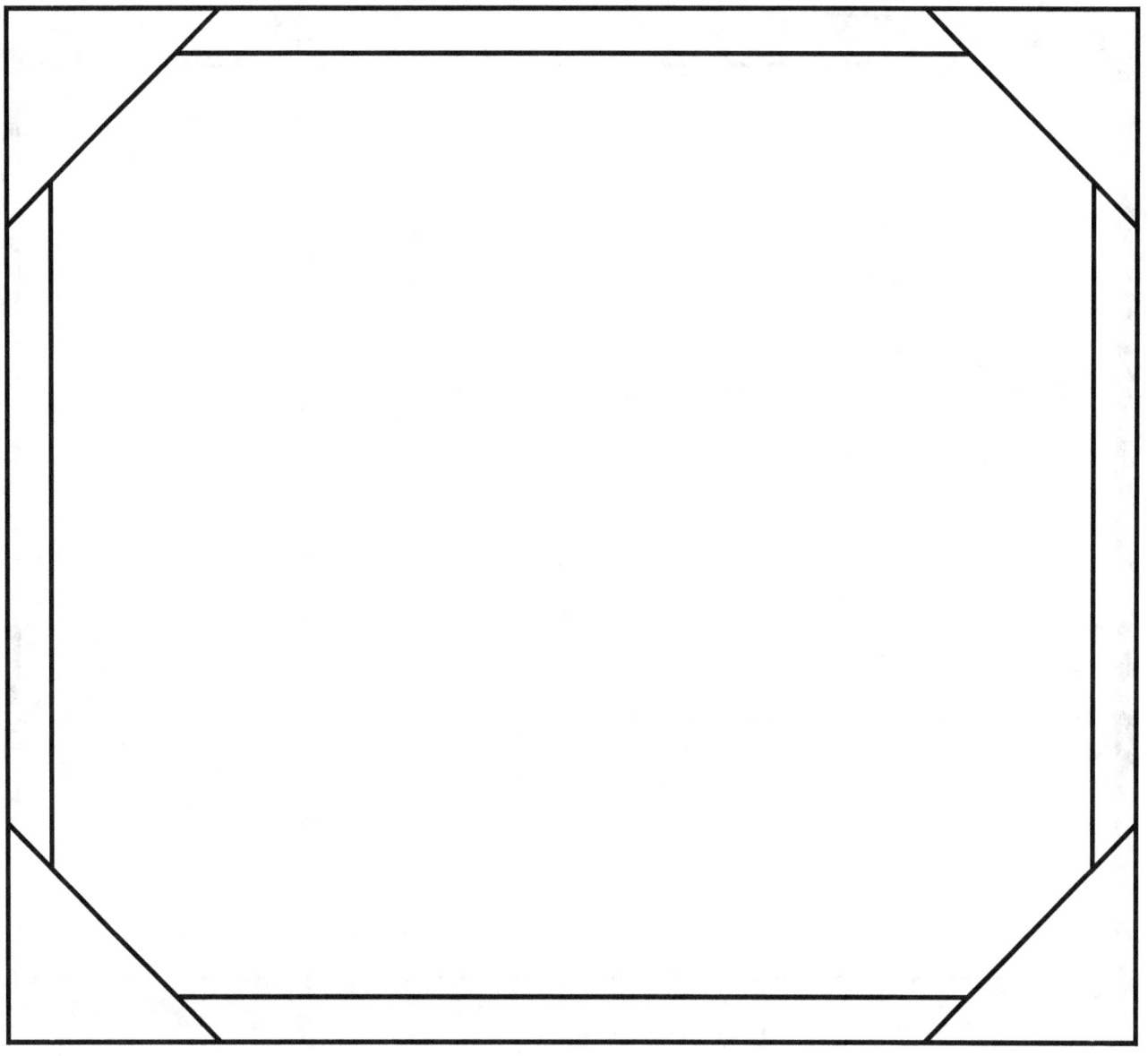

_____

Name

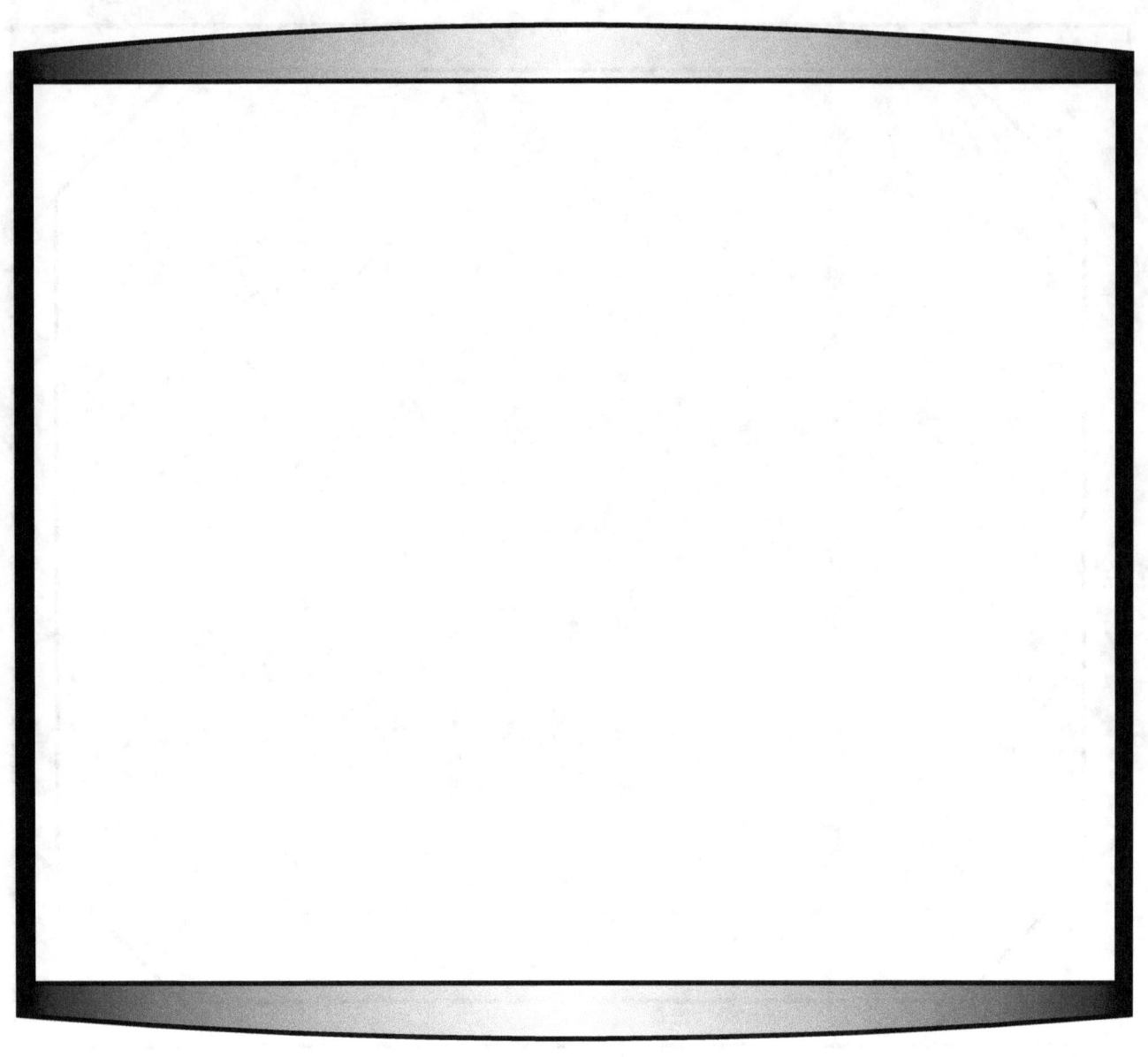

Name _____

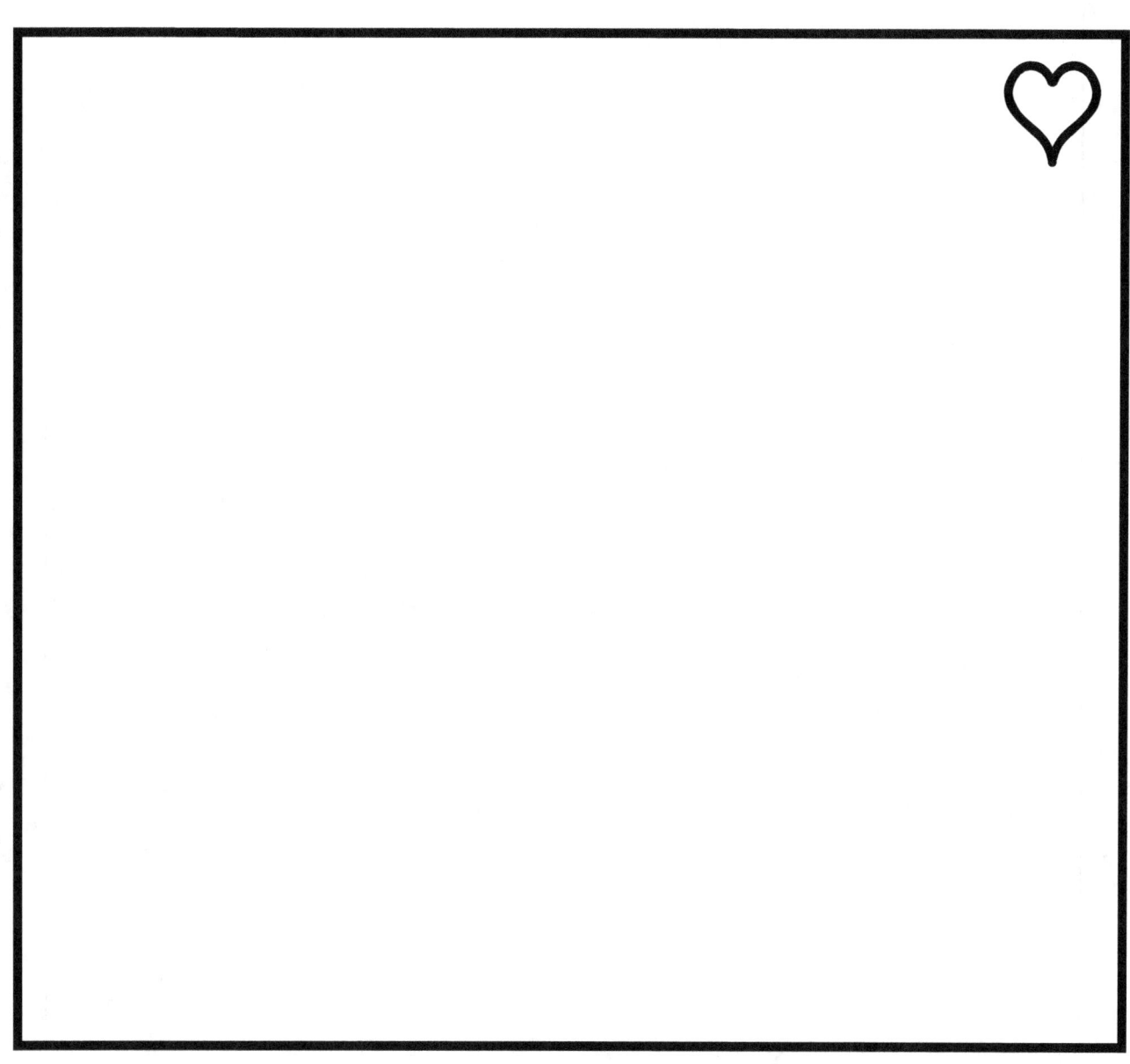

Name

Name

Name

BOOKS by Mark Linley

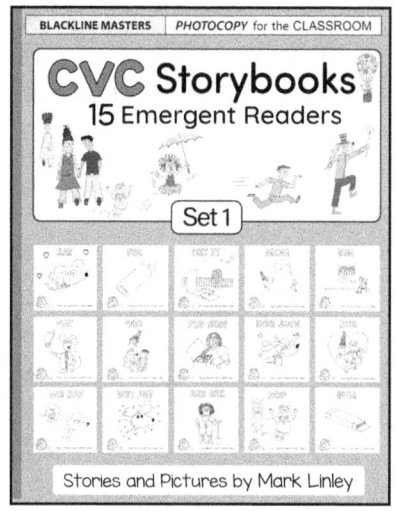

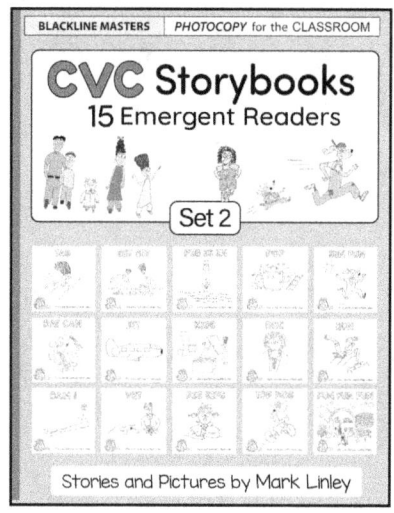

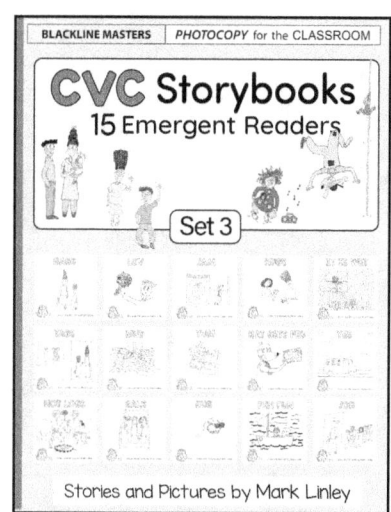

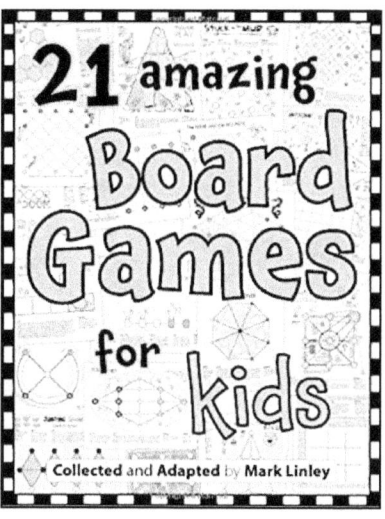

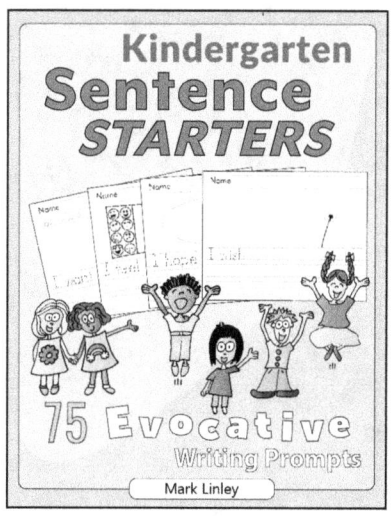

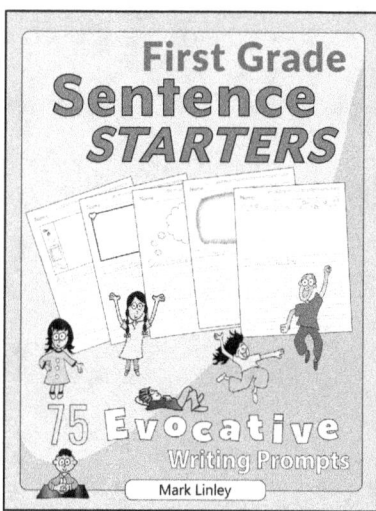

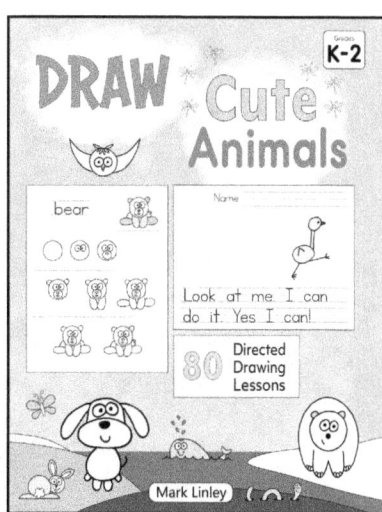

About the Author

Mark Linley is a public school teacher and curriculum developer with over 20 years of experience teaching full time in the primary grades. He is the author of these and many other high quality learning materials, available on Amazon, Barnes and Noble, Teachers Pay Teachers, bartlebysbox.com, and other fine online retail establishments.

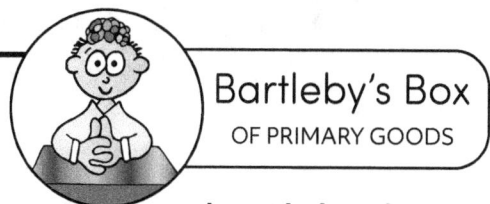

bartlebysbox.com

www.ingramcontent.com/pod-product-compliance
Lightning Source LLC
Chambersburg PA
CBHW081603220526
45468CB00010B/2754